ALLIGATORS
IN THE SEWER

and 222 Other Urban Legends

ALLIGATORS IN THE SEWER

and 222 Other Urban Legends

THOMAS J. CRAUGHWELL

BLACK DOG
& LEVENTHAL
PUBLISHERS
NEW YORK

Published by
Black Dog & Leventhal Publishers, Inc.
151 West 19th Street
New York, NY 10011

Distributed by
Workman Publishing Company
708 Broadway
New York, NY 10003

Designed by Tony Meisel
Book manufactured in Canada

ISBN: 1-57912-061-X

h g f e

Library of Congress Cataloging -in-Publication Data

Craughwell, Thomas J.. 1956-
    Alligators in the sewer : and 444 other absolutely true stories that happened to a friend of a friend of a friend / by Thomas J. Craughwell
        p. cm.
    ISBN 1-57912-061-X
    1. Urban folklore—United States.   I. Title
    GR105 .C73 1999
    398 . 2' 0973' 091732—dc21   98-50123
                                                            CIP

Acknowledgments

Work is rarely fun, but this project was an exception—and I have J.P. Leventhal and Jessica MacMurray to thank for it. When they asked me to write this collection of urban legends, they gave me one of the most enjoyable assignments I've ever had.

I was very fortunate to have Elise Andaya as my editor. She spotted all the details that escaped my notice, and offered suggestions that vastly improved this book.

Finally, my thanks to my friends Kevin Donovan, David Feeney, Teresa Gibbons, Candis La Prade, and Rob Clee and Sandra Sesink-Clee who told me great stories about weird stuff that had actually really happened to a friend of a friend of theirs.

CONTENTS

Introduction

There may be some Americans who could not tell you the name of the vice president of the United States, but virtually every American knows that the sewers of New York City are full of alligators, that the cute little Chihuahua a tourist picked up in Mexico was really a rat and that a foolish woman tried to dry her poodle in a microwave.

These stories are known as urban legends, urban myths or sometimes as modern folklore. Jan Harold Brunvand, the guru of the genre, has defined urban legends as "highly captivating and plausible, but mainly fictional, oral narratives that are widely told as true stories." The tellers usually try to make them plausible by supplying details of time and place that their audience will recognize or by asserting that it happened to "a friend of a friend of a friend of mine."

Like all folklore, urban legends are usually passed by word of mouth, although these days urban legends are just as likely to make the rounds by e-mail. Some legends are told in almost identical versions as far afield as the south of France, South Africa and New Zealand. Urban legends are ubiquitous; everybody has heard some.

Did your mother check the apples you got trick-or-treating for razor blades? When you were in college, did you believe you had to wait 15 minutes if your professor was late for class? How often have you been solicited to help a dying boy who wants to set the world record for receiving get-well cards or business cards? If you traveled to a third-world country, did friends tell you to watch out for suspicious characters who would try to steal your kidneys? All of these are urban legends.

Many urban legends have a distinctly dark cast to them. Fear, paranoia, envy, suspicion of the unfamiliar—all the baser elements of human nature—find an outlet in urban legends. The Murderer in the Back Seat. Abducted by Aliens. Mass Murder on Campus. AIDS Mary. All the stories of young lovers who look for a secluded spot where they can do a little necking and find a grisly death instead. There is no telling how often these urban legends are related around campfires, during slumber parties, over the dinner table or through the grapevine. They are sometimes even reported in newspapers as real events. The plots of these horror legends are fantastical, like something out of Edgar Allan Poe. . . .

Of course, not all urban legends are gruesome. Some legends reassure us that good people get their due (A Good Samaritan Gets His Reward) or that unexpected windfalls do happen (Elvis's Motorcycle). College-based urban legends celebrate the wily student (He Should Have Been More Specific) and take satisfaction in seeing wise guys and cheaters get what is coming to them (Late for Finals and I Like It Better Each Time).

In urban legends people who play fast and loose with accepted social norms usually pay the price. These punishments are often humorous and allow us to laugh at others' foibles. When an executive gets naked in expectation of a liaison with his secretary, his family, his friends and all his business colleagues burst into the room to throw him a surprise party. A white bride never tells her white groom about the one-night stand she had with a black stripper—and nine months later she gives birth to a mixed race child. The only way to free an adulterous wife and her lover from her husband's sports car is to saw off the roof.

While some urban legends reassure us that nobody gets away with anything, others feed our fantasies. A classic example of wish-fulfillment is the belief that Elvis—or Tupac Shakur—is alive. People who believe these legends may be irrational, but they are part of a long tradition of irrationality. Virtually every society believes that one of its heroes is not truly dead but has gone elsewhere and will return to them. For centuries, the English assured one another that King Arthur was regaining his strength on the Island of Avalon and would come back someday to restore the golden age of Camelot. In the 19th century, an Irish urban legend claimed that their great political leader Charles Stewart Parnell was not dead but had slipped away to South Africa where he was still fighting the British as a leader of the Boers. Meanwhile, in England, a similar story was told of the military hero General Gordon who was killed at Khartoum. Many believed that he had escaped into the desert and would soon reveal himself.

Like all folklore, urban legends change over time. A classic example of the evolution of an urban legend is the story of the black man on the elevator who is mistaken for a mugger. In the earliest known version, the man turns out to be Reggie Jackson. Brunvand has collected variants in which the "mugger" is Jesse Jackson or Michael Jackson. Other versions are linked to the increasing popularity of a black performer, such as Eddie Murphy or Lionel Richie. (There is even a bizarre variant in which the "threatening" black man turns out to be Lionel Hampton, the 80-something-year-old jazz musician.) This story is still told today, with Michael Jordan or Mike Tyson in the starring role.

It would be a mistake to adopt the stance of a purist and regard these alternate versions as corruptions of classic urban legends. In fact, variation is an essential component of folklore. After all, these stories aren't memorized verbatim like the Pledge of Allegiance or the Lord's Prayer. Urban legends are fluid, and tellers adapt them to reflect their own era and preferences as well as their fears or prejudices. The legend known as The Enormous Bouffant dates back to the 1960s when that particular hairstyle was very popular. Now that the bouffant has gone out of fashion, it is not uncommon to hear the story told about a middle-aged woman with no fashion sense, a young man with unruly hair or a Rastafarian with dreadlocks. Variation keeps urban legends alive (and they also keep scholars and folklorists in business).

There is an endless supply of urban legends and new ones seem to be cropping up every day. For example, in 1994 Brunvand heard a new story about a gang initiation in which rookies drive around at night with their headlights off, waiting for the first car that flashes its lights at them. They then kill the driver and any passengers. In 1998 I heard a variation on this legend in which gang members killed a deaf man and woman because they mistook the couple's sign language for the hand signals of a rival gang. I wouldn't be surprised if you heard a different version.

THE CURSED MUMMY
AND OTHER
SUPERNATURAL ENCOUNTERS

THE CURSED MUMMY AND
OTHER SUPERNATURAL ENCOUNTERS

The Cursed Mummy

In the late 1890s a party of four well-to-do young English gentlemen made an extended tour of archaeological excavations in Egypt. One evening in the bar of their hotel in Luxor, they met an antiquities dealer who engaged them in a lively conversation about archaeology and some of the artifacts he had acquired over the years.

"In fact," said the dealer, "I've just purchased an exquisite sarcophagus that contains the intact mummy of a princess of the Thirteenth Dynasty. It is the crown jewel of my collection. Would you like to see it?"

The young gentlemen said they were very eager to see the sarcophagus. "Please come to my warehouse tomorrow morning about nine," the dealer said.

At exactly nine o'clock the next morning, the dealer met the four travelers on the narrow street outside his warehouse. "Good morning!" he said as he shook each man's hand. "You're very punctual." Then, drawing a key from his pocket, he unlocked the warehouse door and threw it open. "Please come in," the dealer said.

The dealer led the young men through a labyrinth of wooden

crates to a room at the rear of the building. Inside, standing upright in the middle of the small room, was the princess's sarcophagus. It was eight feet tall and inlaid with gold and semiprecious stones. On the lid was a portrait of the princess herself, her face serene and lovely, and her eyes wide open as if she were still alive.

"It's superb," one of the young men said.

"I think so, too," said the dealer.

For the next hour, the five men examined the sarcophagus closely. The dealer read the inscriptions for them and even opened the lid so his visitors could examine the mummy of the princess.

Then one of the Englishmen cleared his throat and said, "Would you . . . have you . . . considered selling the sarcophagus?"

The dealer seemed taken aback by the suggestion. But now all four of the young men pressed him to sell them the treasure. After some negotiation, the men settled on a price of ten thousand pounds sterling. They each wrote the dealer a check for £2,500 and asked him to have the sarcophagus packed up and sent to their hotel that evening as they were planning to begin their journey home to England the next day.

"Before we conclude our arrangement," the dealer said, "I should warn you that the mummy is said to be cursed. If you are having second thoughts, I will tear up the checks now without any hard feelings."

The gentlemen smiled, and one said, "Thank you. But none of us is superstitious."

Late in the day, the packing crate containing the sarcophagus arrived at the hotel. As three of the gentlemen met in the bar for drinks before dinner, they saw the fourth member of their party walking out toward the desert. They waited for him all that evening and looked for him the next morning. At last they went to the British consulate to report their friend missing. They notified the Luxor police, but a thorough investigation turned up no trace of the missing Englishman. He was never seen again.

From that moment, trouble seemed to haunt the young travelers. One was shot accidentally in the right arm as his servant packed his hunting rifles. Although a surgeon from the British embassy in Cairo came to Luxor to treat the young man, the wound became gangrenous and the arm had to be amputated.

The third man in the foursome found on his return home that bad investments had destroyed his family's fortune.

The fourth man was struck down by an illness which no doctor in England could diagnose or cure.

Remembering the dealer's warning of a curse, the surviving travelers put the sarcophagus up for sale. They found a buyer almost immediately, a London businessman with a passion for Egyptian antiquities.

But no sooner had the sarcophagus been installed in the businessman's home than the curse struck again. His wife and two of his children were severely injured when their carriage overturned. Then the family's house caught fire, destroying every Egyptian artifact in their collection—except the sarcophagus.

Some days later, the *Times* reported that the British Museum had received a superb sarcophagus from an anonymous donor. As two workmen unloaded the sarcophagus in the museum courtyard, one of the men slipped and broke his leg. The other dropped dead two days later.

Now the princess's curse fell upon the British Museum. Night watchmen heard the sound of frantic hammering and sobbing from the coffin. Other artifacts displayed in the same gallery as the sarcophagus were hurled about by some unseen hand. A guard who witnessed the uncanny events died of fright. A charwoman who scoffed at the curse and flicked her dustcloth at the mummy's face lost her only child to a deadly case of measles.

By now, the newspapers had heard of the strange occurrences surrounding the princess's sarcophagus. A photographer who took a picture of the sarcophagus for his newspaper found when he developed the film that the serene image of the princess was replaced by a grotesque, horrifying face. The photographer hurried home, locked himself in his room and shot himself in the head.

The museum's curators ordered the sarcophagus to be kept in storage in the basement. Within days the foreman who had supervised the move was found dead at his desk.

A private collector with an interest in the occult purchased the sarcophagus from the British Museum and then invited the renowned spiritualist Madame Helena Blavatsky to perform an exorcism. After spending a few moments in the princess's presence, however, Madame Blavatsky hurried out of the room, saying, "No one can overcome such evil."

For 12 years, the sarcophagus passed from one owner to the next, leaving behind a trail of disasters and tragedies. Then an American archaeologist purchased the sarcophagus. The curse did not frighten him; he attributed all the misfortunes of the previous owners to the quirks of circumstance. In early April 1912, he arranged for the sarcophagus to be shipped to America and booked a stateroom for himself aboard the same ship—a luxurious new cruise ship of the White Star line that was making its maiden voyage to New York.

The name of the ship transporting the sarcophagus was *Titanic*.

The Bloody Rain

It was almost noon on a hot day in the beginning of July, 1863. For a little over six hours, the slaves had been working in the tobacco fields of the Chandler farm in Tennessee. Mr. Chandler was entertaining a neighbor, Mr. Peyton, on the verandah when several field hands came running up to the house in panic. As they grew closer, Chandler and Peyton could see splotches of what looked like blood on the men's skin and clothes.

At first, the men were too worked up and out of breath to tell a coherent story. But finally one of them blurted out, "It's raining flesh and blood in the tobacco fields!"

The field hands described how a large red cloud had mysteriously appeared over them and covered the field with a gory rain. Although they were skeptical, Chandler and Peyton followed the slaves back to the field and waded into the tall rows of tobacco plants. To their amazement, they saw the tobacco leaves covered with dark red stains. Scattered on the ground were small whitish and grayish fragments that resembled fresh meat.

"It could be a hoax," Peyton said. "But just to be sure, let's collect some samples and take them over to the university in Nashville for analysis."

Chandler sent one of the field hands back to the house for two large cloth sacks. In one they put a few dozen stained tobacco leaves. In the other they put several handfuls of the fleshlike scraps. As they carried the bags of the samples out of the field, both men tried to ignore the putrid smell rising from the bag of fragments.

At the house, they washed up, then mounted their horses and rode to Nashville.

The laboratory of Nashville's Central University's science department was housed in a handsome stone building on Rutledge Hill. Chandler and Peyton found the chairman of the science department, Professor Jackson, told him their story and produced the two sacks.

"That's a wild story, gentlemen," Professor Jackson said.

"We don't believe it rained flesh and blood in my tobacco field," Chandler said, "but I would be obliged if you would analyze these samples for me."

"It will take a few hours to run the tests," Professor Jackson said. "Come back tomorrow and I will give you the results then."

"If it's all the same to you, Professor," Peyton said, "we'll wait."

A few hours later, a student found Chandler and Peyton walking about the campus and invited them to join Professor Jackson in his office. They found the professor standing beside his desk, looking uneasy.

"Well, gentlemen, I confess that I am perplexed by the results of my analysis," he said.

Chandler and Peyton kept silent, so Professor Jackson continued.

"The red stains on the tobacco leaves are most certainly blood."

Professor Jackson paused for a moment before speaking again. "And those fragments are human flesh."

On the ride home, the two men discussed the professor's analysis.

"I still say it's a hoax," Chandler said.

"If I were a superstitious man," Peyton said, "I'd say this rain was a bad omen."

Before long, Peyton's instincts proved to be correct. The next day, both Chandler and Peyton received telegrams announcing that their sons had been killed at Gettysburg.

Variations: Tennessee folklore also tells of a mysterious inky darkness that descended on western Tennessee one day. A legend set in Memphis describes another odd rainstorm in which hundreds of snakes fell from the sky.

The Dying Man

One weekday morning on the North Side of Chicago, as Father Muller was removing his vestments after Mass, a woman appeared in the sacristy.

"Father, could you bring the last sacraments to my son," she said. "I know he will not live through the day. He lives at 1136 West Wellington."

"I'll go now," said the priest. "Wait here while I get the Host and the holy oil."

But when Father Muller returned to the sacristy, the woman was gone.

Nonetheless, he went out to his car and drove to the address the woman had given him. He found a parking spot near the house, walked up the front steps and rang the doorbell.

A healthy-looking young man in his late twenties answered. "Can I help you Father?" he asked.

"I've come to give Last Rites," said the priest.

"You've got the wrong house, Father," the man said. "No one here is sick."

"A woman came to me only half an hour ago, gave me this address and told me a young man here was dying," Father Muller said.

"Father, I'm the only one who lives here, and I'm as healthy as a horse." But as the young man spoke, Father Muller looked over the man's shoulder and saw a photograph on the wall.

"That's the woman who came to see me," he said, pointing to the portrait.

The young man grew pale. "Why don't you come inside, Father."

Together they walked over to the photograph. "I'm certain this is the woman who asked me to bring the sacraments to this house. She said her son would not live to see another day."

"Father," said the young man, trembling now, "this is my mother. She's been dead for five years."

The two men were speechless for a moment. Then the young man said, "Father, maybe you should hear my confession and give me Communion after all."

A few hours after Father Muller had given him the last sacraments, the young man dropped dead of a massive heart attack.

The Devil's Tower

From Route 9 in northern New Jersey, one can see a tall Gothic stone tower. It is all that remains of a grand manor house that was torn down decades ago. Over the years the estate has been divided into lots, so today the decrepit tower rises incongruously at the end of a cul de sac lined with fine new houses.

Residents in the area call the relic the Devil's Tower.

Soon after the mansion was torn down, while the estate was still deserted, the tower caught the attention of a strange cult that mixed druid lore with Satanism. At the solstices and equinoxes, the members gathered at the tower for bloody rites. Children wandering around the empty estate often came across the gory remains of cats and goats.

The holiest day of the year for this cult was Samhain, the day we call Halloween. The druids had believed that on the night of Samhain, the barriers between earth and hell were removed and demons and the souls of the damned walked among the living.

"They are hungry for blood," the cult's leader told his band of followers. "And we will feed them."

In the days before Halloween, members of the cult began to visit the local high school, looking for a suitable victim. They wanted a girl—tall, clear skin, beautiful. Then they spotted Laura, the high school's homecoming queen.

On the afternoon of Halloween, several of the cult members drove to the high school in a black truck. They watched Laura leave the school with several friends. Driving very slowly, the cult followed the girls at a distance. One by one, Laura's friends went down side streets to their own homes. When Laura was alone, the driver accelerated and pulled the truck onto the sidewalk in front of her, blocking her way. Before the girl knew what was happening, three men grabbed her and threw her into the back of the truck. They gagged her and tied her hands and feet while the driver turned the truck toward Devil's Tower.

That night, at midnight, when all the trick-or-treaters were safe in their beds, while the police went door to door through the town looking for anyone who had seen Laura, as Laura's frantic parents waited for some scrap of hopeful news, the cult gathered in the tower. They laid Laura on a cold stone slab, cut out her heart and splashed the walls of the tower chamber with her blood.

The next morning, when the police finally came to the tower, they found Laura's body. But the cult had vanished and were never seen in the area again.

Since that day, anyone who comes to the Devil's Tower on Halloween night will see a frightening apparition. At midnight, out of the mist emerges the ghostly form of a beautiful girl, dressed in a blood-soaked gown and screaming for someone to save her.

Variations: Some versions of the story say that if you walk backwards around the tower six times at midnight, the devil will appear.

The Light in the Church Tower

On a warm summer night in July 1921, a young couple walking along Pavonia Avenue in Jersey City, New Jersey, saw two pale lights in the bell tower of St. Joseph's Church.

"Look," said the woman. "There are lights on in the tower."

Her boyfriend glanced up. "Maybe it's a signal for Paul Revere," he said.

"Don't make jokes," the woman said. "They're eerie. They look like cat's eyes."

Soon more people along the avenue stopped to stare at the strange lights. As the crowd grew larger, one of the parish priests came out of the rectory.

"What's going on here?" he asked.

"See for yourself, Father," answered a man in the crowd as he pointed up to the tower.

"It's nothing," the priest said. "Someone's left the lights on in the tower. I'll go turn them off myself."

But by the time the priest got to the top of the tower, the two lights had disappeared.

Night after night, the "cat's eyes" appeared in St. Joseph's tower. The sexton of the church decided he would get to the bottom of the mystery. He posted guards at the foot of the tower stairs. But they saw no one enter or leave. He removed all the light bulbs from the fixtures in the tower. But the cat's eyes still appeared. He scattered flour on the floor of the bell chamber. But whoever or whatever had been in the tower left no footprints.

The pale glimmering cat's eyes appeared for nine nights, and on the ninth night, the eyes showed a bloody red streak.

Standing among a crowd of spectators on the sidewalk, the church sexton said, "That's it. I'm going to the belfry."

The next morning, the church sexton was found sitting in the choir loft, dead. The cat's eyes disappeared and were never seen again.

The Prophetic Videotape

A newlywed couple went to San Francisco for their honeymoon. They filled up their days sightseeing and shopping, and every night they enjoyed long, leisurely dinners in the city's best restaurants. But after a week of nonstop activity, the couple were exhausted.

"Let's stay in tonight," the wife suggested. "The suite has a VCR, and there's a video store around the corner. We can have room service bring something up."

"Sounds good to me," the husband said. "I'll go get a movie. Do you have anything in mind?"

"Get something romantic," the wife said. "Rent that Demi Moore–Patrick Swayze movie."

"You mean *Ghost*?"

"Yeah," the wife said. "I'd like to see *Ghost*."

After dinner in their room, the couple stretched out on the bed to watch the video. The movie ended. The credits had finished rolling. But the husband couldn't find the remote to rewind the tape. Suddenly, Patrick Swayze appeared on the screen.

He looked straight at the woman on the bed and said, "Call your mother."

Then the screen went blank.

"That was weird," said the husband.

"Yeah." After a moment the wife said, "Maybe I should call home."

"What are you going to say? 'Hi Mom! Patrick Swayze said I should give you a call?'"

"Okay. It's weird. But I have a funny feeling about this."

"Forget about it," the husband said. "It's just some strange trailer."

"I guess," the wife said.

The husband rewound the tape while the wife put the tray of dinner dishes outside the door of the suite.

The next morning, while the wife was getting dressed, the phone rang.

The husband called from the bedroom, "Honey! Your brother wants to talk to you."

The wife picked up the phone. "Eddie? Is everything okay?"

"I'm sorry to do this to you," her brother said. "But you've got to come home. Mom died last night."

Variations: In a variant of this legend the movie is *Always* and the star who speaks to the woman is Richard Dreyfus. When the husband takes the video back to the store, he tells the staff about the strange "trailer." They check the tape the man rented as well as every other copy of *Always* in the store, but none of them have the eerie message from Richard Dreyfus.

Three Men and a Ghost

Studio executives deny this story completely. They insist the scene in question was filmed on a set in Toronto, not in a New York City apartment.

The 1987 movie *Three Men and a Baby* was filmed in various locations in New York City. One scene involving Ted Danson and Celeste Holm takes place inside a New York apartment. Behind the actors is a window, and in the window, standing behind a sheer curtain, is the indistinct figure of a little boy. Strangely enough, no one spotted the mysterious figure when the movie was playing in the theaters, but thousands have seen it on videotape.

The little boy is wearing jeans and a T-shirt. He is absolutely motionless. And leaning against the wall beside him is a rifle. At no time in the scene do Danson and Holm interact with the boy. They do not even seem aware that he is in the room with them. Nor does the little boy appear at any other point in the movie.

The cast and crew of *Three Men and a Baby* were mystified when they were shown the image on the videotape. And since the apartment was vacant when they rented it for the movie, they did not know who to turn to for a solution.

Finally, it was the superintendent of the building who solved the mystery. Not long before the movie was filmed there, he said, a little boy living in the apartment had accidentally shot and killed himself with his father's hunting rifle. His distraught parents could not bear to live in the place where their son had died, so they moved out of the apartment.

"I saw the parents yesterday," the super said. "They came by to see me. They had just rented *Three Men and a Baby*." Then he paused. "That's their little boy in the movie."

Mass Murder on Campus

One Halloween afternoon, Geraldo Rivera brought a renowned psychic onto his talk show. In the course of the interview, Rivera asked his guest, "Most of your predictions are for the distant future. Do you see anything we should be concerned about today?"

The psychic concentrated and then she said, "There's a university in the Midwest. It's a Big Ten school. I see a statue of Abraham Lincoln on a hill. There is a large lake at the foot of the hill. The school's name begins with 'W.' And I see red."

"Wisconsin," Rivera said. "Wisconsin's colors are red and white."

"No," said the psychic, "not the red of school colors. I see the red of blood. There's a murderer loose on the Wisconsin campus at Madison. And before the night is over, 12 students will be dead."

In Madison, the psychic's prediction caused a panic. Students who had planned to join the huge outdoor Halloween celebration on State Street that evening now ran for their cars and got out of town as fast as they could drive. Other students barricaded themselves in their dorms. Sponsors of the State Street Beer Bash announced that the party was off. But one of the fraternities refused to be intimidated. Halloween in Madison was one of the biggest events of the year, and the brothers were not going to miss it because some psychic had predicted mayhem on campus. The guys let it be known that the party in their frat house was still on.

By nine o'clock, about 40 fearless partiers were doing shots in the frat house's cellar bar overlooking Lake Mendota. It was a small turn-out by Madison standards, but the hardy few were determined to have a good time anyway.

As the night wore on, one by one, the guests slipped off to find empty beds and sofas where they could pass out. By three in the morning, a dozen partiers remained in the cellar bar. The last one awake was the frat's president. He unlocked the sliding glass doors and stepped out onto the lakefront terrace. He was pretty drunk and he thought a little fresh air would clear his head. Then, after a few moments, he went back into the house, collapsed in a ratty recliner and fell asleep.

Late the next morning, one of the hungover brothers woke up in his room. The house was freezing. He stumbled downstairs to see if the heater's pilot light had gone out in the night. In the cellar bar he found the sliding doors to the lakefront terrace wide open. Twelve bloody corpses were scattered around the room.

Variations: Virtually every college has a version of this legend and tailors the details to fit the school. In its original form, Jeanne Dixon, the renowned psychic of the 1960s, predicts the murders.

The Phone in the Crypt

A wealthy man named James Ball had a morbid fear of being buried alive. When he had his mausoleum constructed in Boston's Mount Auburn Cemetery, he arranged for a telephone to be installed in his crypt.

In time, Mr. Ball died. His widow, accompanied by a great crowd of relatives, friends and business associates, followed Mr. Ball's body to the grand limestone tomb.

After the funeral, Mrs. Ball gave a lunch for the mourners at the Ball mansion. By sundown, the last guests had gone home and Mrs. Ball was alone.

Just after dark, the phone rang.

A maid passing outside the sitting room heard Mrs. Ball say, "Hello?" Then she heard a blood-curdling scream. The maid rushed into the room and found Mrs. Ball sitting upright in a chair, clutching the telephone, a look of horror frozen on her face. The maid took the phone from Mrs. Ball's hand and put the receiver to her own ear. The line was dead, and so was Mrs. Ball.

An autopsy concluded that Mrs. Ball had died of a massive coronary. But the identity of the caller remained a mystery.

On the day of the funeral, the same crowd of mourners gathered and once again followed a body to the Ball mausoleum. When the crypt was unsealed, the crowd saw that the lid of Mr. Ball's casket was open. And the telephone was off the hook.

The Graveyard Wager

Variations on this story have been in circulation since the Middle Ages.
Five girls had gathered at a friend's house for a slumber party. Behind the house was the town graveyard. Jessica, the girl hosting the sleepover, had a clear view of the cemetery from her bedroom window.

"Could you see Old Man McCluskey's funeral yesterday from up here?" one of the girls asked her hostess.

"Yeah," Jessica said. "It was pretty boring. But things got a lot more interesting after everybody went home."

"What do you mean?" her friend asked.

"I think they buried Old Man McCluskey alive."

Erin, the most outspoken of Jessica's friends, made a face. "That's really stupid," she said.

"No. Seriously," Jessica said. "I've been watching the grave. And the dirt keeps moving around. Like something underground is trying to get out."

"The ground's probably just settling," Erin said.

"No," Jessica insisted. "I think Old Man McCluskey was really buried alive."

"I still say you're goofy," Erin told her friend.

"Well, if you don't believe me," Jessica said, "I dare you to go out to the grave right now and—" She looked around the room; her skis caught her eye. "And drive this ski pole into the grave."

"Yeah!" one of the other girls cried. "He'll probably grab it and make you pull him up!"

"That's so stupid," Erin said. "What will that prove?"

"I think you're chicken," Jessica said.

All the other girls joined in, crying, "Chicken! Chicken!" and "Dare! Dare!"

"All right!" Erin said at last. "I'll do it."

"We'll turn off the light so we can see you," Jessica said.

Erin put on her shoes, grabbed the ski pole and slipped out the back door of the house. From the window, her friends saw her climb over the fence and then she was swallowed up in the darkness of the graveyard.

They waited. Minutes went by. Then an hour. Then another

hour. The girls waited all night for their friend to come back. In the morning they ran to the parents' room.

"Erin's gone! Old Man McCluskey killed her!"

The parents got up, dressed quickly and everyone ran out the back of the house to the graveyard. There, on the freshly dug grave of Old Man McCluskey, lay the body of their friend, facedown in the dirt. She had driven the ski pole through the bottom of her nightgown and pinned herself to the grave. The ground around her was churned up from her desperate efforts to pull herself free from the ski pole.

The thought that Old Man McCluskey had caught her had frightened poor Erin to death.

Variations: Alternate versions of the legend feature a drunk who drives a stake through the hem of his overcoat, a braggart soldier who plunges his sword through his long cloak or a person who hammers a nail into a wooden cross and pins himself to the grave marker.

Bloody Mary

Mary Worth is said to have lived in Massachusetts in the 17th century. Her face was hideously disfigured by dark red scars. Children in the village called her "Bloody Mary," and followed her through the streets chanting her name over and over.

During one of the colony's witch scares, Mary was accused of being in league with the Devil and was hanged. One night, not long after Mary's execution, a group of children decided to play at conjuring. They set up a mirror against the wall and sat in a semi-circle around it. Then they all began to chant, "Bloody Mary, Bloody Mary." When they had chanted the name for the 99th time, Mary appeared in the mirror. Her face was more hideous than ever. Her hands had turned into claws. She reached through the looking glass to tear the children's faces.

Shrieking and screaming, the terrified children tumbled out of the room.

Although Bloody Mary disappeared that day, her spirit remains, waiting for someone to call her name.

Variations: In some places children chant, "I do believe in Mary Worth." In other parts of the United States the spirit's name is Mary Whales, Mary Johnson or Mary Lou. Some folklorists believe there is a connection between the Bloody Mary legend and the Chicano legend of La Llorona, a weeping ghost who wanders forever searching for her children whom she murdered.

The Jersey Devil

People in southern New Jersey have been scaring each other with stories of the Jersey Devil since 1735.

A teenage girl in southern New Jersey was left alone for the weekend while her parents went to the casinos in Atlantic City. On Saturday night, a terrible storm swept into the area. A heavy rain pounded on the roof. The wind rattled every window. And a bolt of lightning knocked out the power in three counties.

All alone in a dark house lit only by candles, the girl was very frightened. But she had her dog with her—a big golden retriever. He wasn't exactly a killer, but at least he was comforting.

When she was ready to go to sleep, the girl took the dog into her room with her and had him lay down beside her bed. Every time thunder crashed over the house, she awoke and reached down her hand. "You still here, Boo?" The dog would lick her hand and the girl was reassured that she was not alone.

Eventually she fell into a deep sleep. At about six in the morning, something dripping in the bathroom woke her. She climbed out of bed and went down the hall. There was her dog, hanging by its neck from the shower head. Scrawled on the mirror in blood was the message, "The Jersey Devil can lick hands, too."

Variations: Dozens of grisly stories are told about the Jersey Devil.

He is said to have caught a babysitter one night and hacked off her arms and legs. When he sees young lovers parked in remote spots, he lures the boyfriend out of the car, kills him and suspends the body over the roof. Other legends claim that he climbs into the back seat of a car and murders the driver with a razor-sharp pruning hook.

Mothman

The Mothman stories first appeared around Point Pleasant, West Virginia in 1966.

The Mothman is a manlike creature with a 10-foot wingspan and huge red eyes. He was a worker who was severely injured in an accident at a chemical plant in West Virginia. Instead of dying from his injuries, he mutated into a giant moth. He haunts remote country roads, especially dead ends where lovers go to park.

Most kids around Point Pleasant know better than to stray into Mothman territory. But there are always a few skeptics.

One such kid, a high school football star, scoffed at the Mothman stories and drove his girlfriend to a secluded spot off a county road. Just as the guy started to make his move, his girlfriend saw a large shadow pass over the car.

"It's him," she screamed. "Let's get out of here."

"It was probably just a hawk. Take it easy."

He kissed her, and she relaxed a bit. But then there was a thump on the roof of the car.

"Please. Pleeeeze. Let's go."

"Why? Because some dead branch fell out of a tree? Come on. We finally have some time to ourselves."

The guy put his arms around his girlfriend. Then there were scratching sounds on the roof of the car.

The girl began to scream.

"Okay. Okay. Calm down. I'll go take a look. But you're going to feel dumb when I show you it's just branches again."

"No! Don't go outside. Just drive me home. I want to go home. Right now."

"I'll be back in a minute. Lock the doors if it makes you feel better."

As the girl locked the car doors, she heard one final thump on the car roof, as if something heavy had been dropped on it. And then nothing.

A minute passed. Then several more. The guy did not return, and it was deathly quiet outside the car. The girl was on the verge of panic. She didn't have the keys to drive away and she didn't have the courage to get out of the car herself. She didn't know what to do. So she leaned on the car horn.

Out on the county road, a state trooper heard the horn and followed the sound of it down the dead end where he saw the car.

The trooper came up to the car on the passenger side and motioned to the girl to roll down the window. Before she could say anything he told her, "Miss, you need to stay in the car until I can get some help."

But the girl would not stay inside. When she stepped out, she saw her boyfriend sprawled atop the roof of the car. Someone, something, had ripped open his chest and eaten his heart.

Variations: Gruesome accidents in chemical plants have produced a host of bloodthirsty monsters, including the Green Man of central Pennsylvania, Hyrum the Ax Murderer in the mountains of Utah and the Lizard Man of South Carolina.

The Well to Hell

Newspapers in Finland were the first to report this story as an actual event. From there, it has spread around the world.

Engineers working on the Kola Peninsula in Siberia were drilling a well, searching for oil or natural gas. In addition, they found rare geological formations and even gold. Eager to discover what else the well would yield, they kept drilling.

After more than a year, the well was about 1,800 miles deep. Then one day, the drill bit suddenly began to rotate wildly. The geologists and engineers felt a blast of searing heat gush out of the hole and thought they heard faint sounds emanating from the well.

They raised the drill and lowered temperature gauges to measure the heat at the bottom of the hole. It registered over 2,000 degrees Fahrenheit.

"We've penetrated to the molten center of the earth," one geologist said.

"But that doesn't account for the sounds," one of his colleagues said.

So they lowered highly sensitive microphones down the hole. Up from the well came the sounds of agonizing screams.

"We haven't penetrated the earth's core," the geologist said. "We've entered the gates of Hell."

Variations: An alternate version sets the story at an Alaskan oil rig where 13 workers were killed when the devil came roaring out of Hell.

The Image in the Glass

An elderly woman had been bedridden for many years. Her only pleasure was looking out the window beside her bed. Her neighbors grew accustomed to seeing her sitting up amid her pillows, a shawl around her shoulders and her lacy nightcap on her head, watching the activity in the street.

One evening, there was a tremendous thunderstorm. The elderly invalid saw a lightning bolt strike a tall pine tree beside her window and shatter it to splinters. The woman must have felt the shock of the bolt, for she fell into a coma.

She lingered through the night and passed away quietly the next day without ever regaining consciousness.

The woman's nurses asked her friends to come and prepare the body for burial. When they entered the bedroom and approached the bed, they were astonished to see a clear image of the old woman in the windowpane. It was a perfect likeness of her—just like a photograph. She was propped up among her pillows in her shawl and cap, looking intently out the window, just as she had for years.

Variations: In some versions of this legend, the image in the glass is the portrait of a prisoner who spent many years in a cell, staring out his window. In another version, the image is the portrait of someone who was murdered in that room. And in some accounts of the legend, the image is a miraculous portrait of Jesus or Mary.

The Dead Body in the Car

On a dark night in December 1941, a couple were driving along a country road in Indiana when they saw a hitchhiker. He was a middle-aged man dressed in a trench coat and wearing a fedora. As the car came closer, the hitchhiker pushed his hat back on his head;

the headlights lit up his handsome face.

"Should we pick him up?" the husband asked.

"He looks very nice," said his wife.

The husband stopped the car and rolled down his window. "Where are you going?"

"Fort Wayne," said the hitchhiker.

"That's on our way," the husband said. "We can drop you off."

As the hitchhiker climbed into the back seat he said, "Thanks for the lift. Where are you folks heading?"

"We're going to stay with my sister in South Bend for a few days," the wife said. "She's been scared to death since the attack on Pearl Harbor."

The three travelers made small talk until they arrived at the outskirts of Fort Wayne. "You can drop me off anywhere along this road," the hitchhiker said.

Once he was out of the car he said, "Thanks again. Look, I have no money, I can't pay you anything for your kindness. But I can answer any question you care to ask me."

The husband shot a mischievous look at his wife. "Any question at all, huh? Okay, sport. Tell us when the war is going to end."

"The war will end in August 1945," said the hitchhiker.

"August 1945," the husband repeated. "You're sure about that."

"As sure as I am that you will have a dead body in your car before you reach South Bend." Then the hitchhiker turned and vanished into the night.

"Did he say we would have a corpse in the car tonight?" the wife said.

"He's a loon," said the husband. "Don't pay any attention."

Several miles later, the couple saw an accident up ahead.

"Jeez, what a night," said the husband.

"Pull over! Pull over!" the wife said. "Somebody might be hurt."

"My God," said the husband. "It's an ambulance." Before he could stop the car, a paramedic ran up shouting, "I have a patient here. He's severely injured. You have to get us to the nearest hospital."

As they placed the injured man in the back seat, the paramedic said, "I'll direct you. Drive as fast as you can."

As they pulled up to the hospital, a half-dozen nurses, orderlies and doctors hurried out the door with a gurney to receive the patient. The husband and wife followed them all inside.

It was only a matter of minutes before the ambulance paramedic and an attending physician joined the couple in the waiting room. "It was good of you to try to help," said the doctor. "But I'm afraid he died on the way here."

The Ghost Pilot

A commercial airplane pilot with 30 years' experience was flying a 747 from Chicago to Los Angeles. One of the flight attendants on board was his daughter.

During the course of the flight, the plane suffered one problem after another. The pilot did everything he could to compensate for the mechanical failures. His daughter, in the meantime, tried to keep the passengers calm.

Finally, she had a spare moment and slipped into the cockpit. "Daddy, tell me what's going to happen," she said.

"It's serious," her father answered. "We can't get to any airport. I'll have to make an emergency landing in one of those fields down there."

"We're all going to die, aren't we," the daughter said.

Her father looked her straight in the eye. "I promise I will never let anything bad happen to you."

His daughter went back and prepared her passengers for the landing.

As they descended, the pilot could barely keep control of the aircraft. Then the landing gear failed. The 747 hit the ground hard. One of the wings broke off and the plane swung around wildly before it came to rest.

Among the passengers there were a few lacerations, plenty of bruises and one or two broken bones. But everyone was alive. It was a different story in the pilot's cockpit. In the impact the pilot's neck had been broken. He was dead.

The daughter was grief-stricken. But she was also proud of her father for having saved the lives of more than 200 people.

Several years later, the daughter was preparing a plane for take-off. As she stepped into the galley she saw her father's ghost. "Get off this plane. There's trouble with the engines. If the ground crew doesn't correct the problem, this plane will crash."

Frightened, the woman hurried off the plane, found the foreman of the mechanics and convinced him to inspect the engines one last time. The foreman found a fault in the engine which would have caused the plane to explode on takeoff.

The young woman's father had kept his promise: He had saved her life again.

The Phantom's Warning

On a cold wet night in the 1920s, a man named Hugh Hamblen walked along a mountain road. He was heading for the hospital where his son had been taken after the police pulled him out of a wrecked car.

The road was slick with rain and heavy fog made it impossible to see more than a few feet ahead. Yet time and again cars flew past

Hamblen at high speeds, impervious to the bad road conditions and the bad weather.

At a turn in the road Hamblen saw another car barreling along. As it came closer, Hamblen froze—it was skidding sideways. It was not going to make the turn.

The car hit Hamblen and tossed his body against the guardrail. By the time the ambulance arrived, Hamblen was near death. His ribcage was shattered and both of his lungs were punctured.

He lingered for two days at the hospital before finally succumbing to his injuries.

Since then, on stormy, foggy nights, drivers have seen Hugh Hamblen standing along the side of the mountain road, signaling them to slow down.

Taking Laurie Home

A young man home from college for the weekend went to a dance at a church hall. While he was standing around the refreshment table, talking with his friends from high school, he saw a young woman standing at the threshold, watching the dancers. She was beautiful. Her blonde hair fell over her shoulders. She wore a white dress that must have come from a vintage clothing store.

"Who's that?" he asked his friends.

They turned, looked and shrugged their shoulders. They had

never seen her before.

"I'll catch up with you guys later," the college boy said. He headed over to the vision standing in the doorway.

"Hi! My name's Tony. Do you want to dance?"

The girl smiled slightly and nodded her head.

Tony took her hand and led her onto the dance floor.

"Your hands are cold," he said.

"I'm cold all the time these days," the woman answered.

"Excuse me for asking, but I don't know your name," Tony said.

"It's Laurie," she answered.

"Are you new in town? I grew up here, and I've never seen you around before tonight."

"My place is outside town," Laurie said.

Laurie was not much of a talker, but Tony was smitten with her nonetheless. At about eleven o'clock, Laurie said she had to go home.

"I'll drive you," Tony said.

As they walked across the parking lot to Tony's car, Laurie shivered and said, "I'm so cold."

"Here," Tony said. "Take my jacket." He draped it over Laurie's shoulders and held the car door open for her.

Laurie directed him to a farmhouse about 10 miles outside of town. She would not let Tony walk her to the door, and stood at the curb until she saw him drive away. But a few minutes later, Tony realized that Laurie still had his jacket. He went back to the house and knocked on the door. An elderly man answered.

"Good evening," he said. "I just dropped Laurie off, but I forgot to get my jacket back from her."

The elderly man sighed. "It happens every year."

"Sorry?"

"Laurie died 20 years ago on this very night. Every year she comes back and spends a few hours among the living. I don't know where your jacket is."

Tony could hardly believe what he had heard. But some strange force seemed to draw him to the cemetery. With a flashlight, he wandered among the graves. At last he found Laurie's. His jacket was neatly folded and lying on top of her headstone.

Variations: A ghostly apparition who tries to return home is one of the most prolific of all legends. Among the variants are stories of a bride who waits for her dead lover, a Woman in Black who was cruel to her slaves and spends eternity haunting her old plantation and a little girl who died in a theater fire and waits in the balcony for her parents to come and take her home.

THE SCUBA DIVER IN THE FOREST FIRE AND OTHER STRANGE DEATHS

The Scuba Diver in the Forest Fire and Other Strange Deaths

The Scuba Diver in the Forest Fire

For days, brushfires ravaged the dry hills of southern California. When the fires were out, firefighters found the body of a diver in full scuba gear in the middle of the charred wasteland.

They turned the body over to forensic investigators, but the conclusions of the autopsy were mystifying.

"The diver did not burn to death," the chief of forensics said. "He drowned."

"You're saying he drowned in the middle of a brushfire? How is that possible?" the fire chief asked.

"We gave this some thought," the chief of forensics said. "You called in firefighting helicopters that haul water out of the ocean and dump it on the fire, right?"

"Right."

"Once the scoop is full, it seals itself automatically, right?"

"Yeah. So?"

"We figure one of the helicopters must have scooped this guy up when he was scuba diving in the ocean. He ran out of oxygen during the flight. With no way to get out of the scoop, he drowned.

The helicopter got to the site and dumped its load of water, and the diver went down with it."

Variations: Versions of this legend have cropped up from southern California to the south of France. Sometimes he is a scuba diver, while in other versions he is a snorkeler. In some accounts the body of the diver is discovered caught in the branches of a charred tree.

The Flying Chevy

At the bottom of a sheer cliff in the middle of the desert, two officers of the Arizona Highway Patrol came upon a vehicle shattered beyond recognition. About 100 feet up the cliff face they spotted large chunks of metal embedded in the rock wall.

"Looks like a small aircraft," one of the cops said.

"Look again," said his partner. "It's got four wheels. This was a car."

"Okay. But where's the driver?"

There was no trace of a body. And searching the area, they found no sign that someone had walked away from the wreck (not that anyone could have survived the crash).

First the cops radioed for a wrecking company to come and collect the debris. Then they notified a forensics lab.

A week later the chief of forensics sat down with the two high-way patrol officers who had found the wreck.

"We found parts of a Chevy Impala," he said, "and parts of a solid-fuel rocket identical to the type the military uses to give their aircraft an extra boost at takeoff."

"You're kidding," the first cop said.

"Not in the least. In fact, by studying the wreckage and visiting the site, we were able to piece together the rest of the story.

"It appears that the driver took his car out to the desert, to a long, straight stretch of road. It was probably there that he attached the rocket to his car. We found the spot where the driver fired up the rocket—the asphalt showed signs of having melted. This was about three miles from the scene of the crash.

"A solid-fuel rocket achieves its maximum thrust in five seconds—which means the Chevy was traveling at 350 miles per hour. Not surprisingly, the driver tried to reduce his speed. We know this because we found traces of the destroyed brakes and the four blown tires half a mile from the crash site.

"Then there are no more signs of the car on the road. We surmise that at this stage the Chevy was airborne. Seconds later, it hit the cliff, approximately a hundred feet above the ground. That accounts for the parts of the vehicle you saw embedded in the rock above the wreckage. The rest of the shattered vehicle fell to the ground."

"And the driver?" the first cop asked.

"We recovered some fragments of bone and hair."

"That's all?" said the second cop.

"There were also bits of fingernail embedded in a piece of debris which we believe was part of the steering wheel."

The Airborne Lawn Chair

A truck driver who had always wanted to learn to fly but could never get around to taking lessons came up with a unique alternative. An inveterate tinkerer who was always working on some odd invention in his garage, he was certain that his ingenious flying machine would get him into the record books.

One Saturday morning his neighbors saw him anchoring his favorite lawn chair to the ground. Then he went into the garage and came out carrying 50 deflated weather balloons and rolling a large tank of helium. He called to his neighbors, "You guys want to give me a hand here?"

As the neighbors collected in his yard, the truck driver assigned them jobs. "You fill the balloons. You tie them off. You secure them to the lawn chair."

"Mike, what are you doing?" one of the neighbors asked.

"I am going to pilot the first flying lawn chair," he answered.

"You're out of your mind."

"Nope. I've figured the whole thing out. These weather balloons are strong. I should have no trouble getting off the ground. And my own weight will keep me from flying too high. It should be a nice, graceful flight over town. I can't wait to see the looks on people's faces as I drift over their houses."

"So how do you get down?" the neighbor asked.

Mike rummaged in a large backpack strapped to the back of the lawn chair and pulled out a pellet gun. "When I'm ready to make my descent, I'll shoot out the balloons one by one and make a perfect landing.

"In case anything goes wrong, I've got this." He reached into the backpack again and pulled out a parachute. "Plus I've got my cell phone. I'll be okay. And I'll make history."

By this time, the neighbors had finished tying the weather balloons to the lawn chair. Mike took his seat, strapped himself in with leather belts, and said, "See you all later!"

Then he cut the moorings that anchored the lawn chair to the ground.

Mike had been right: the weather balloons were strong. He and his chair shot up a few thousand feet into the air at a surprising speed. He was terrified. First he vomited over the side of the chair. Then he got out his pellet gun and shot out a few of the balloons to slow his ascent.

As planned, the flying lawn chair began to lose altitude. Then

Mike lost his grip on the pellet gun.

He fumbled with his cell phone and dropped that, too. He was still about 100 feet in the air—not high enough to use the parachute, but far too high to jump. And aside from waving and yelling to people as he drifted over their yards, he had no way to call for help.

A stiff breeze came up and began to push Mike and his lawn chair farther and farther away from home.

Soon he was outside the town, in open country. No houses, no businesses and not even much traffic on the roads. That was worrying, but not nearly as worrying as the high-voltage power lines that were stretched across the path of the flying lawn chair.

With his hands trembling, the frantic "pilot" tried to untie some of the balloons. But his neighbors had followed his directions and secured the balloons tightly to the chair, and Mike hadn't thought of bringing a knife to cut the cords.

A few seconds later, the driver of a passing car saw the flying lawn chair, propelled by the wind, move swiftly toward the power lines that ran alongside the highway. He saw the man in the chair lean back and extend his legs, as if that would enable him to veer away from the wires. Then there was a sharp sound of crackling electricity, followed by a roar as the helium balloons exploded into flames. In his rearview mirror, the driver saw the burning lawn chair crash to the ground.

The Deadly Log Flume

A new amusement park had opened in Florida on the edge of the Everglades. During the hot Florida summer, the most popular ride was the log flume.

Half a dozen high school kids came to the park one blistering day in August. They waited in line for the flume for over an hour, and finally their turn came to climb aboard the ride.

"I can't wait to get soaked," one guy said to his girlfriend. "I'm burning up."

His girlfriend said, "My mom says if you put your wrists in cool water, it lowers your body temperature."

"It's worth a shot," the guy said.

As the ride started to move, he plunged his arms into the water. "This feels great," he said.

A moment later he yanked his arms out of the water, yelling, "Something bit me!"

His friends saw small puncture wounds all over his arms. They yelled to the flume operator, "Somebody's hurt! Let us off!" But their car was too far along. It had to go through the first circuit of the ride.

The car flew around the track, then slowed and began to climb the chute that was the climax of the ride. The kid said to his girlfriend, "My arms feel like they're on fire." Then he fell unconscious.

As the car went over the crest of the chute, his girlfriend began to shriek.

By the time the car came to a stop, the boy's arms were swollen and discolored. He was barely breathing.

The park's emergency medical team rushed him to a local hospital, but the boy died on the way. An emergency room doctor took the kids into his office. "I don't understand this. Your friend died of snake bites. It was my understanding that you kids were at an amusement park."

Meanwhile, the management of the amusement park had shut down the log flume. They drained all the water from the ride. In the canal just past the ride's starting point, the park's safety inspectors discovered a large nest of poisonous water snakes.

Snake Lake

After several days of heavy rains, Alabama's Guntersville Lake over-flowed, covering fenceposts and tree stumps that under normal conditions were many yards from the water's edge. On the first sunny day after the rainstorms, a group of college kids decided to spend the day waterskiing on the lake.

At first, the kid piloting the speedboat was careful to stay clear of the shallow water. But by the end of the afternoon, the skiers had become more and more daring. Finally, in what was supposed to be the last run of the day, the boat's driver made a wide turn and the skier swung into the shallow end of the lake, barely missing a shattered tree stump that jutted above the lake's surface. Something below the surface snagged one ski and the skier tumbled into the water. When he came up, he found himself ensnared in a tangle of barbed wire. He thrashed around in the water trying to get himself free. He shouted to his friends for help and cursed as the wire spikes pricked his skin.

Then the occasional pinpricks became sharp, agonizing stings as dozens of poisonous water snakes sank their fangs into the skier's flesh. By the time the boat filled with the skier's friends got to him, he was screaming in pain and terror. The water was churning with the frenzy of the snakes and the skier's frantic efforts to escape. Worse still, his friends were too frightened by the mass of snakes to reach into the water and haul him to safety in the boat.

He died in the water, while his frightened friends watched helplessly.

Variations: Another version tells of a boy who jumps into a pond and lands amid a mass of water snakes. Before he dies, he manages to warn his friends not to come near the water. The most grisly variant of this story involves small children who play in a sandpit filled with snakes.

The Giant Catfish

Something was clogging one of the channels that released water from the bottom of the dam at the Tuttle Creek Reservoir in Arkansas. The foreman of the dam's maintenance crew hired a team of three divers to see what the problem might be.

They had only been gone a few moments when two of the divers almost exploded out of the water, sputtering and gasping for air, trying desperately to climb out of the water.

"What's wrong?" shouted the foreman. "What's happened? Where's the third guy?"

The two divers talked at once and made no sense.

"Huge!"

"It's the size of a truck!"

"It bit him in half!"

"What are you telling me?" the foreman said.

Shaking uncontrollably, almost crying from fear, one of the divers said, "There's a huge fish down there. An enormous catfish. The size of a car. It's at the bottom of the dam, blocking the channel. It must be eating everything the current carries its way."

"And it just ate Harry," the other diver said.

"You're out of your minds," the foreman said.

"No. The fish bit him in half. He's dead."

"Bull—" the foreman began. But as he looked over the railing, he saw a dark reddish stain on the water. And then a human leg bobbed up to the surface.

Variations: Almost every dam and lock in the United States has a story of a giant fish that devours swimmers or maintenance men. There are even tales of marine monsters lurking near oil rigs off the coast of Texas and swimming amid the wreckage of the USS *Arizona* in Pearl Harbor.

The Bug in the Ear

The origins of this very popular story have been traced back to England about the year 1000.

While a woman was sleeping on the beach in California, a tiny earwig climbed into her ear and burrowed forward. Several days later, the woman went to her doctor complaining of a terrible earache.

After peering into her ear, the doctor sat back. "I can't see anything," he said. "Let's see what an X-ray can tell us."

When the film came back, the doctor sat down with his patient and her husband in his office.

"Now I want you to stay calm. An earwig is burrowing through your ear canal. We can't get to it. The only thing we can do is to wait a couple of weeks until it makes its way clear through your skull. It will climb out of your other ear and you'll be fine."

Of course, when the woman heard this news, she was not fine. She became hysterical. It took her husband and three nurses to hold her down just so the doctor could give her a tranquilizer.

"We'll hospitalize her and keep her heavily medicated for the next couple of weeks," the doctor said to the husband. "That should help her get through this."

Sure enough, about two weeks later, the earwig crawled out of the woman's ear. The husband was at his wife's bedside when the tiny creature appeared. He grabbed it and put it in an empty water bottle. The next day, the couple, with the earwig in the bottle, sat down with the doctor for a final examination.

"Let's get another set of X-rays," the doctor said.

It took a little longer for the film to return this time. When the X-rays finally arrived, the woman, her husband and the doctor all assembled in the office once more.

"I'm afraid I have to modify my diagnosis," the doctor said. "I've examined the earwig and the X-rays." He took a deep breath. "This was a female. It must have been pregnant when it crawled into your ear canal. It's laid its eggs in your skull. When the eggs hatch, the young earwigs will devour your brain."

Variations: It is thought that the name "earwig" gave rise to the belief that these insects liked to crawl into human ears. The idea that the bug ate its way through the head and out the ear on the other side, or laid its eggs inside the skull, is a later embellishment that was dramatized in the 1970s television series, Rod Serling's *Night Gallery*.

The Good Luck Tee

A devoted golfer moved to a new town in Connecticut. Once they got to know him, his neighbors nominated him for membership in the local country club which was famous for its especially challenging golf course.

One evening, a neighbor dropped by the newcomer's house. "You're in," he said. "You can start playing first thing tomorrow morning if you like."

The new member was the first one at the links the next day. He was thrilled by the beauty of the course. The grass was thick, lush and free of any kind of weed. He had never seen a golf course so magnificently tended.

After he teed off, he picked up the tee and put it in his mouth. At every hole, he used this tee. "I always do this for luck," he told the other members. "This will be my new good luck charm."

He played 18 holes of golf the first day. The next day he returned for another 18 holes, once again using his lucky tee. As he walked happily from hole to hole, he chewed and sucked on the lucky tee, as if he were ingesting its good luck.

On the third day, the golfer wasn't feeling well, but he couldn't keep away from the links. He played badly, and he felt worse. Yet he struggled from hole to hole, the lucky tee stuck between his clenched teeth.

At the 13th hole, the golfer dropped dead.

An autopsy showed that he had died of poisoning. A follow-up lab report on the lucky tee found that it carried a lethal amount of pesticide—the type the country club's groundskeeper used to kill weeds.

Variation: In another version of the story, the golfer is a military man who dies, not from a lethal dose of pesticide, but from a severe allergic reaction to a supposedly harmless weedkiller that has been spread on the golf course. The legend ends with the golfer's widow winning a $20 million lawsuit against the manufacturer of the weedkiller.

The Ancestral Boots

An old Texas rancher was rounding up stray cattle when a rattle-snake reared up and bit him through his boot. He had nothing he could use to treat himself, so he applied a tourniquet, climbed on his horse and headed for home.

Through the kitchen window, the rancher's wife saw him coming. Even from a distance he looked strange. His head was bowed and the reins were slack in his hands. A few minutes later, the horse and rider arrived in the front yard, but the old rancher did not climb down off his horse. When his wife and the hired hands got to him, they found that he was dead in the saddle.

"Imagine him having a heart attack and not even falling off his horse," said the rancher's son.

The morning after the funeral, as the son was getting dressed, his mother came into his room. "These are Daddy's boots," she said. "I thought maybe you'd like to wear them."

The son took them and put them on his feet. They pinched a little, but he didn't say anything about it to his mother. He didn't want to hurt her feelings. Besides, they'd probably stretch after he'd worn them for a couple of days.

At the end of the day, the son came riding into the yard of the ranch, slumped over his horse. Like his father, it appeared that he had had a massive heart attack out on the range.

The morning after the son's funeral, the old rancher's wife came into her eldest grandson's room. Her face was pale and drawn. "Your Grandpa wore these boots for twenty years," she told the young man. "Your Daddy only got a chance to wear them for one day. Do you want them?"

The grandson said yes, and put them on. The boots were too tight, but he couldn't complain about it to his grandmother after all she'd been through.

At the end of the day, the grandson came riding into the yard of the ranch, slumped over his horse, as dead as his father and his grandfather.

A few days later, the grandmother called her youngest grandson to her. On the floor beside her were the boots. She was weeping. "Your Grandpa always said these boots were good luck. I'm beginning to think they've cursed us. Take them out and burn them for me."

The boy picked up the boots, and as he did, he saw something sticking out just above the heel. He carried the boots out to the tool shed, took a pair of pliers and pulled at the object embedded in the boot. He expected it to be a thorn. Instead, out came a rattlesnake fang still filled with venom.

Variation: In a modern version of this story a rancher runs over a rattlesnake with his truck. Some of the snake's fangs are embedded in one of the tires, so the rancher drives to his mechanic's shop to have them pulled. The careless mechanic is scratched by the fangs and dies.

No News but Bad News

One of the earliest printed versions of this grim legend appeared in 1879 in McGuffey's Fifth Eclectic Reader.

After being away on business for several weeks, a well-to-do man began the journey home. As he neared his farm, he met his steward on the road.

"So, steward, what's new at home?" he asked.

"Sir, I'm afraid your dog has died," the steward replied.

"How could that happen? He was barely two years old."

"He gorged himself on burnt horseflesh, sir."

"Where did he find burnt horseflesh?"

"Sir, I'm sorry to say that all the horses died when the barn burned down."

"How did the barn burn down?"

"A spark from the house blew onto the barn roof. We were so busy trying to save the house we didn't notice that the barn had caught fire until it was too late."

"My house burned down?" the man asked in horror.

"Yes sir. One of the candles set around your wife's coffin was placed too close to the window curtains. The curtains caught fire, then the whole house went up in flames."

"My wife is dead? Did you say my wife is dead?"

"She died of a seizure, sir. After your eldest daughter ran off with the hired man."

The man groaned and covered his face with his hands. When he regained his composure, he said, "My wife is dead. My daughter's run off. My house is gone. The barn is gone. My horses and even my dog are dead. Where am I to live with the other three children?"

The steward cleared his throat.

"I wouldn't worry about that, sir. They all perished in the house fire."

The Elaborate Suicide Attempt

After his business failed and his wife left, a man decided to kill himself, but he wanted to be sure that he wouldn't botch the operation. After some thought, he decided that hanging would be the best method. He found a tree with a stout limb reaching out over the edge of a cliff 50 feet above the sea and chose this spot for his suicide.

Although he was eager to leave this world, he did not want to feel any pain. So he collected a few dozen sleeping pills.

Of course, sleeping pills don't work immediately, and the man had read terrible stories of people who had taken half an hour to die at the end of a rope. He decided to shoot himself, too—just to be on the safe side.

On the day he decided would be his last, the man took the rope, the sleeping pills and the gun to the cliff. He swallowed the sleeping pills. He tied the rope to the branch and slipped the noose around his neck. He put the gun to his head and as he stepped off the edge of the cliff, he fired.

But the sudden drop threw off the man's aim. The bullet missed him completely and cut through the rope instead. The man plunged into the sea where he swallowed so much seawater that he vomited up the sleeping pills.

He swam ashore and resolved not to attempt suicide again.

The Funny Smell

This legend was dramatized in the 1995 movie Four Rooms.

A couple went to Las Vegas for a few days of vacation. Once they were in their hotel room, they detected a peculiar smell.

"I'll call the desk and get a different room," the husband said.

"No," the wife said. "I don't want to change rooms. I like the view from here. Just call housekeeping. They'll take care of the problem."

While the couple went down to the casino, a maid inspected the room, but she could not find the source of the odor. She sprayed air freshener in the room and left.

When the couple returned to their room, the smell was no better. They called housekeeping again and went out for dinner.

Another maid came to the room. She searched for any spills or food that might have been left lying around. When she found nothing, she sprayed the room with air freshener and left.

Late that night the couple came back and found that their room still stank. This time they decided to search the room themselves.

"It's strongest near the bed," the wife said.

"Maybe somebody wet the mattress," said the husband.

They stripped the blankets and sheets off the bed, and lifted up the mattress. There, in the platform that served as the frame of the bed, they found the decomposing corpse of a prostitute.

Shrink-to-Fit Jeans

On a Saturday night in the late 1970s, a sophomore at a New Hampshire college put on a pair of new jeans and went to a party at a frat house. By midnight, he was profoundly drunk. On a trip to the bathroom, the bathtub looked so cool and inviting that he climbed in and promptly passed out.

The next drunk to use the bathroom thought this was comical. From the bathroom door he yelled, "Hey! You gotta see this!"

A handful of partiers crowded in around the tub.

"He must be really wasted."

"Next time, remind me to sleep it off in his bathtub."

Then the only girl in the group said, "You know, it's a shame he didn't think to fill the tub first."

Everyone looked at her as if she were out of her mind.

"Seriously. If you wear new jeans and soak in them in the bathtub, they shrink to the shape of your body. They look really good."

One of the guys said, "Then let's do this guy a favor and shrink his jeans for him!" He plugged the drain and turned on the water.

With the type of seriousness only drunks can summon up, the little group stood and watched as the tub filled. When the water was chest high, they turned off the taps.

"He's going to be so grateful in the morning," the girl said as everyone filed out.

About noon the next day, one of the frat brothers staggered out of bed into the bathroom. The frat's houseguest was still in the tub.

"C'mon. Wake up!" he shouted.

But the kid in the tub didn't move.

"Let's go. Time to get up." He splashed some water in the drunk's face, but still he got no response.

"Look, you gotta sleep it off somewhere else. People want to use the shower." He shook the guy; the body was deathly cold.

"Oh shit!" he exclaimed.

The frat brother called 911. Minutes later, a crew of paramedics with their paraphernalia crowded into the bathroom.

"He's dead, isn't he," the frat president said.

"Yes he is," one of the paramedics said. "Who put him in a bathtub filled with water?"

"One of the girls who was here last night said it would make his jeans shrink to fit his body."

"Yeah, it did that," the paramedic said. "The jeans shrank so well they cut off his circulation. It killed him."

Variations: In an alternate version of this legend, a young woman dies when she purposely soaks in a bathtub filled with water so her jeans will be as tight as possible. Another variant claims that the woman does not die, but is mortified when the police and ambulance crew have to cut her out of her too-tight jeans.

The Cask of Excellent Brandy

The roots of this legend go back to an historical event: In 1805, the British Navy packed Lord Nelson's body in a cask of rum to preserve it and shipped it back to England for a state funeral.

In London, a young couple bought an old house that had once served as a tavern. There was an old wine cellar in the basement, filled with empty casks. The barrels were too large to fit through the cellar door, so the husband and wife broke them up and carried out the pieces. When the cellar was almost empty, the husband found a last cask hidden in the corner.

"This cask is still full," the husband said.

"You get a tap," the wife said. "I'll get a couple of glasses. Maybe the wine or whatever is still good."

To their delight, the couple discovered that the cask held excellent brandy.

"I've never tasted anything like this," the husband said.

"It must have aged down here for a hundred years," the wife said. "What else could account for this incredible flavor?"

For years, the couple celebrated every holiday and every important family occasion with a decanter of their prize brandy. They served it to their friends at the conclusion of all their dinner parties. The fame of the brandy spread, until an editor of a British food and wine magazine asked if the couple would agree to be the subject of an article.

The magazine sent a connoisseur of brandy and cognac to the couple's house. They took him down to the old wine cellar and poured him a glass of their brandy directly from the cask.

The connoisseur held the glass under his nose and inhaled. "The bouquet is remarkable," he said. Then he took a small sip and rolled it around on his tongue. "Wonderful. Wonderful! My friends, this is a unique 18th-century brandy. I have never tasted its like. If I were to advance a supposition, I would suggest that this brandy was distilled at a long-vanished French vineyard. Perhaps one destroyed during the Revolution. May I have another glass?"

The couple could not have been more pleased, although after the article was published, they were besieged by "connoisseurs" eager to sample their remarkable brandy.

Finally, after giving them many years of pleasure, the cask ran dry.

"Let's save the cover of the cask and the tap as a memento," the wife said.

The husband agreed that it was a fine idea. Together they went down to the cellar to break up their prize cask.

They swung their mallets together and loosened the cover. The husband set his mallet down, grabbed the cover and wrenched it free.

A moment later, out spilled a skeleton, still wearing scraps of 18th-century garb.

Gloomy Sunday

In 1933, a new song, "Gloomy Sunday," debuted on radio stations in Hungary.

> *Sunday is gloomy, my hours are slumberless.*
> *Dearest, the shadows I live with are numberless.*
> *Little white flowers will never awaken you,*

Not where the black coach of sorrow has taken you.
Angels have no thought of ever returning you.
Would they be angry if I thought of joining you?

It was rumored that the songwriter's girlfriend had committed suicide; this melancholy ballad was his attempt to express his grief. The song was so popular that it spread to America, where Billie Holiday sang it in nightclubs. But just as the song was becoming an international hit, radio stations in Europe were instructed to stop playing the song.

Since the debut of "Gloomy Sunday," government officials had noticed a sharp increase in suicides. Often family members and friends of the victims found suicide notes that made reference to "Gloomy Sunday" or quoted some of its lyrics. The situation was particularly bad if the song was played on a rainy Sunday: The next morning, the morgues of major European cities would be filled with corpses.

One by one, the nations of Europe banned the song. The United States joined the "Gloomy Sunday" ban when government officials saw a rise in the American suicide rate.

Meanwhile, the composer of "Gloomy Sunday" was in desperate straits. Royalties from his hit song dried up. No one would publish any of his new music. And the possibility that his song had been instrumental in the deaths of hundreds of people on two continents tormented him constantly.

The composer slipped into a deep depression. He stopped writing. He would not leave his apartment. He refused to see his friends. The only person with whom he had any contact was the delivery boy from the grocer.

One day, when the delivery boy came to the composer's apartment with his bags of groceries, he heard the composer playing the piano. He recognized the song at once—it was "Gloomy Sunday." He stood in the hallway for a few minutes, listening. The song came to an end. There was a pause. And then a gunshot rang out in the apartment.

Dying to Get into the Movies

During the making of the 1926 version of *Ben-Hur*, several scenes were filmed in Italy. The movie's famous sea battle between Roman soldiers and pirates was shot at the seaport of Livorno. The director needed hundreds of extras, so he hired local residents to play these parts. The only requirement was that they had to be able to swim.

The scene would be magnificent. Several Roman galleys had been built for the battle and were anchored offshore. The extras were outfitted in replicas of Roman armor, including heavy metal breastplates and helmets. The cameramen and the director were on modern boats anchored on the perimeter of the Roman ships.

The director shouted, "Action!" and the battle began.

Everything was going perfectly. The costumed residents of Livorno put their hearts into the fight. The special effects people had arranged for a few fires to break out on the Roman galleys to create even more excitement. But on one of the galleys, the fire got out of control and began to spread through the entire ship.

Frightened extras jumped into the sea to escape the flames.

"This is great!" the director said.

"No it's not!" said his assistant. "Look out there! Some of the extras are having trouble swimming. Stop the filming so we can pull them out of the water!"

One of the cameramen looked at the director.

"Keep the cameras rolling!" the director commanded.

"But they're drowning!" the assistant said.

"I can get more extras for ten dollars a head. But this scene is costing me a hundred grand!" As several of the extras sank beneath the waves, the director yelled to the cameramen, "Keep the damn cameras rolling!"

The Lethal Hospital Room

The nursing staff of the intensive care unit in a hospital in Johannesburg dreaded Friday mornings. Week after week, whoever was placed in Room 713 would be found dead first thing on Friday.

The hospital administrators launched an extensive investigation of the room, from the air-conditioning ducts to the single electrical outlet that powered the life-support system. But the investigators found no sign of airborne viruses, no trace of faulty wiring, no indication of power surges. Nothing. In fact, one investigator commented on the cleanliness of Room 713. "They don't just clean the floors," he said, "they polish them."

If the investigators were baffled, the staff of the intensive care unit was uneasy. What was going on in Room 713?

In the absence of any rational explanation for the strange deaths, the nurses decided among themselves that they would no longer assign patients to Room 713. But one day intensive care became so crowded with new patients the staff had no choice. Someone would have to go to Room 713.

Early on Thursday evening, the senior nurse of the night shift assembled her staff. "Tonight, we're all going to take a one-hour shift in Room 713. I've worked out a schedule. No nurse leaves that room for any reason. If the experts can't figure out what's going on, then we'll solve this mystery ourselves."

Hour after hour, all night long, the nurses took their turns sitting with the patient in Room 713. By nine in the evening, all the visitors had gone home. By midnight, even the most restless patients were asleep. The only sound in Room 713 was the gentle hum and hiss of the life-support system.

The last shift in the room ended at six. It was Friday morning, and the patient in Room 713 was alive. The nurse who had had the last watch of the night stood, yawned, stretched. She wished "Good morning" to the cleaning lady who was rolling her floor polisher into Room 713.

As the nurse headed to the lounge for a cup of coffee, the cleaning lady reached down to the room's only electrical outlet. She unplugged the cord that ran to the life-support system and plugged in her floor polisher. The whir of the polisher drowned out any other sounds in the room. The cleaning lady did not hear the patient convulse in his bed. Why should she? She had never heard any of the others.

The Embarrassed Family

The 91-year-old patriarch of a large family in Taiwan was dying. His eight children, their spouses and all the grandchildren assembled at the family home in order to be present when the old man passed into eternity.

A day or two after the clan had assembled, the patriarch took his last breath. The mother of the family, who had been calm throughout the crisis, broke into hysterical weeping. She grabbed her husband's body and tried to lift him. She tore at her hair and scratched her face. It took all four of her daughters to physically restrain their grief-stricken mother and lead her from the death chamber back to her own room.

All night long, the widow howled and shrieked until, an hour or so before dawn, emotional exhaustion overcame her grief and she fell asleep.

Her children were distraught. Her grandchildren were terrified. So the eldest son called a family conference while their mother slept. "I have never seen Mother like this," he said.

"I don't think anyone has ever seen Mother like this," said his eldest sister.

"Nor should anyone," the eldest son said. "That's why I think we should go to the herbalist and get a sedative so Mother will be able to control her emotions at the funeral."

The suggestion made good sense to everyone. No one wanted the embarrassment of seeing their mother carry on in this manner at their father's funeral.

The next day, the eldest daughter went to the herbalist's store. The herbalist was an old friend of the family. He sympathized with the daughter over the loss of her father, and seemed genuinely shocked to hear that her mother had lost control of her emotions.

"This will calm your dear mother," he said as he handed a small bottle to the woman. "It's a strong sedative, but if you put five drops in a pot of tea that will dilute it. After she drinks one cup, she will be herself again. Calm, but alert. Remember—five drops. No more."

The daughter thanked the herbalist and hurried back to her parents' house.

The next morning was the day of the funeral. The house was in confusion as more and more relatives and friends arrived to pay their last respects. The eldest daughter was determined to prepare her mother's tea herself, but she endured constant interruptions. Newly arrived mourners asked to see her. Her children seemed unusually demanding. Her husband couldn't find his best shoes.

At last, she had a moment to herself. She took out the small bottle from the herbalist and put five drops in her mother's teapot as the herbalist had instructed. But given her mother's condition, it really didn't seem to be enough. So she added three more drops to the tea. She was about to screw the cap back on the bottle when she heard her mother begin to weep hysterically once more. "Well," she thought, "a couple more drops can't hurt."

Finally, with ten drops of the sedative in the tea, the daughter carried the teapot and a small porcelain cup to her mother's room.

Her mother was wrapped in a dressing gown, sobbing in a chair beside the window.

"Good morning, Mother. Did you get any rest last night?" the daughter asked.

The grief-stricken woman did not say a word; she just gestured to her daughter to leave the tea on a table beside the bed.

The daughter kissed her mother on the forehead and left.

Two hours later, the entire family was ready for the funeral, but the mother had not come out of her room yet.

Her daughter went up to get her. She stood at the door and knocked. There was no answer. She called softly, "Mother?" There was no response. She called more loudly, but her mother still did not come to the door.

At last, the daughter opened the door. Sitting in a chair beside the window was her mother, cold and dead. On the bedside table was the teapot, completely empty. The old woman had drunk every drop of the overdosed tea.

The Enormous Bouffant

The bouffant was the most popular hairstyle in the mid-1960s. Some girls prided themselves on their ability to tease their hair and stiffen it with hairspray into a very high bouffant. One woman at a college in Mississippi had a bouffant that was almost two feet high.

To keep it intact, she slept sitting upright in bed and wrapped it in plastic before she stepped into the shower. Her hair was washed only once a month when she went to the beauty salon.

One warm spring day, just after she had returned from an appointment with her stylist, the girl decided to take a walk in her college's botanical garden. As she passed under a flowering dogwood tree, her bouffant caught a spiderweb hanging from the branches. The woman never noticed.

Three weeks later, while she was sitting in class, she felt something warm and wet trickling down her forehead. She touched it with a tissue. It was blood.

She excused herself from class and was on her way to the college's clinic when she collapsed. A passersby hurried to her assistance, but the woman was unconscious. By the time the paramedics arrived, a pool of blood had collected around the woman's head and her bouffant was matted with blood.

A physician and two nurses met the ambulance at the emergency room entrance.

"What have you got?" the doctor asked.

"It's a head wound. But we can't find the source."

"Let's get her into Trauma One. And cut off that hair!"

With the first snip of the scissors, a massive nest of spiders spilled out of the bouffant. It was pandemonium in the trauma room as the spiders leapt onto the doctors and nurses, swarmed over the woman's body and scurried across the floor.

Later, after the orderlies and hospital maintenance crew had the spider infestation under control, the trauma crew returned to examine the corpse. They cut off the rest of the bouffant and scraped away the spiders' nest. Underneath it was a hole the size of a dime where the spiders had eaten through the woman's skull and into her brain.

Variations: In some versions, the young woman becomes mysteriously ill and it takes the doctors some time to determine the cause of her malady. Once the bouffant went out of style, the subject of the story became a middle-aged woman with no fashion sense. In some versions, the protagonist is a young man with long unkempt hair.

Demon Alley

Off Route 23 in northern New Jersey is a road where no car or truck has gone for many years. The asphalt is crumbling and potholed. Weeds and tall grass grow from cracks in the pavement. Every other tree along the abandoned road bears a No Trespassing sign. People who live in the area call this road Demon Alley.

At the end of the road are a few dozen wooden houses. All the doors are padlocked. All the windows are boarded up. It's obvious that the houses have been empty for years, yet the buildings are pristine. No one has spray-painted graffiti on the walls. No one has pried the boards off the windows or broken the padlocks on any of the doors. No one would dare break into any building on Demon Alley.

In the 1920s this was a growing neighborhood. Then a stranger moved into one of the houses, and odd things began to happen. Pets disappeared. If a little girl left her doll outside, she would find it later with its head missing. The incidents were beginning to make the residents uneasy. Then the newcomer suggested that they hold a neighborhood meeting to discuss the problem. Since his house was the largest on the street, he invited everyone to meet there the next evening. "Bring the entire family," he said. "There's plenty of room. We'll turn it into a party."

The next day, after sundown, every man, woman and child walked over to their neighbor's house. Once everyone was inside, their host locked the front door. Suddenly, men and women in heavy black hooded robes burst into the room. They wielded large knives, meat cleavers and axes. Within minutes, they had massacred all of the helpless residents.

It was a local police officer cruising through the neighborhood who first suspected that something was wrong. At six in the evening, not a single light was on in any of the houses. When backup arrived, the cops began investigating the houses, one by one. Everything was orderly and tidy in every house on the street. There was no sign of violence anywhere—until they came at last to the largest house on the street. The drapes had been drawn; they could not see in the windows. All the doors were locked, so the police had to break into the house. In the large front parlor, they found the bodies of the dead—hacked, disfigured and dismembered.

The identity of the newcomer and his followers remains a mystery. They vanished the night of the massacre. Police investigators speculated that the murders had been committed by a Satanic cult, but no one was ever arrested or charged with the crime.

The Gunslinger

An obnoxious little man from Newark moved out to Tombstone, Arizona. Surrounded by traces of the Old West, he began to fancy himself a gunslinger. He bought a six-gun and drove out to the desert to teach himself how to shoot.

Day after day he returned to the desert to practice. His favorite targets were giant saguaro cacti. He imagined that they were desperadoes and he was John Wayne. There was one saguaro in particular he liked to use for target practice. It was massive: 15 feet high and 4 feet around at the base, with two huge arms that made the cactus look like it was surrendering to the Newark cowboy. After a couple of months of taking potshots at this cactus, it was chewed up by bullet holes. But the marksman never gave a thought to the damage he was inflicting on the cactus.

One day, as usual, he drove out to the desert to indulge in his favorite fantasy of saving the life of Cameron Diaz from a 15-foot-tall outlaw. He blasted away at his saguaro. When he stopped to reload, it seemed to him that the saguaro swayed slightly. Curious, he walked over and saw that the base of the cactus was soft and spongy—almost rotted through. It wouldn't take much to make this giant fall over.

As he contemplated the loss of his favorite adversary, a new gunslinger appeared in the desert. This one came from East St. Louis and he, too, saw himself as a hero of the Old West. But while the Newark cowboy favored a six-gun, this character had bought a shotgun. He saw the giant saguaro cactus, but not the small man who was standing behind it. He took careful aim, pulled the trigger and caught the saguaro in the middle.

It wobbled for a moment, then lurched backward.

The man with the shotgun heard a high-pitched "No!" as the saguaro fell. When he ran over he found the gunslinger from Newark, crushed beneath the giant cactus.

Skin-So-Tight

A woman who had been overweight all her life resolved one New Year's Eve that she would lose 100 pounds by the next New Year's Eve. Her friends thought that was too ambitious a goal, but the woman was determined. She checked herself into a weight-loss spa and began a six-month regimen of exercise and carefully prepared low-fat meals. By the end of the six months, she had lost 50 pounds. The woman was jubilant, but it was not enough. She had set 100 pounds as her goal.

She left the spa, returned to New York City and hired a chef to ensure that she ate properly and a personal trainer to design an effective exercise program for her. In the remaining six months she succeeded in shedding another 50 pounds. But when she looked in the mirror, the woman was not pleased by what she saw. After being overweight for so many years, her skin was stretched and flabby. So she sought out the best plastic surgeon in New York.

"Tightening the skin to your new body is a simple procedure," the surgeon assured her. "You'll be pleased with the results."

After surgery the woman was indeed delighted by what she saw. Her skin clung to her new lean and firm body as if she had exercised all her life.

But even thin people experience setbacks. The woman's boyfriend left her for a 20-year-old underwear model. She made risky investments and lost a fortune, which forced her to sell her home in the Hamptons.

In her depression she turned to the one thing that had always consoled her. Food. For several weeks it seemed that she did nothing but eat. The woman's skin stretched itself to the limit, trying to accommodate the new weight, but the plastic surgery had left no place for these fresh deposits of fat to go. One night, as she was working on her third pint of Heath Bar Crunch ice cream, the woman exploded.

When she failed to appear at her office for several days, concerned friends went to her apartment. They convinced the building's doorman to open the apartment for them. They found the woman's ruptured body in the kitchen, where the walls and floor were splattered with bits of Heath Bar Crunch.

NAKED AT HIS OWN
SURPRISE PARTY AND
OTHER SEXUAL ESCAPADES

Naked at His Own Surprise Party
and Other Sexual Escapades

Naked at His Own Surprise Party

An executive at IBM turned 40, and all day long members of his staff and his colleagues dropped by to wish him a happy birthday. His assistant, a beautiful 25-year-old woman, came into his office last. "I'd like to buy you lunch today," she said. "Something special. Just the two of us at that romantic little French bistro on 55th Street."

The executive agreed, of course. At noon, he and his assistant slipped out of the office and headed for the restaurant. She ordered champagne, and they lingered over their meal for more than two hours.

As the waiter served them coffee and dessert, the assistant said, "Did you know that I live on this block?"

"I had no idea. That's very convenient—for getting to work, I mean."

"Yes, it is convenient," the assistant said. "In fact, why don't we get the check and then drop by my place for a drink."

A few minutes later, they were in the assistant's apartment. As she fixed the drinks, she spilled club soda on her skirt. "I'd better change," she said. "You wait here, and when I get back we'll have an afternoon you'll always remember."

Thinking he was about to get lucky, the executive stripped off all his clothes. But no sooner had he stretched out naked on the couch than he heard a loud cry of "Surprise! Happy Birthday!" The bedroom door burst open, and there were his wife, his kids and all of his colleagues from the office.

Variations: A husband organizes a surprise party for his wife. To get her out of the house, he takes her to a restaurant for a romantic dinner. When they return home, the wife goes upstairs to get ready for a night of lovemaking, while the husband smuggles the guests into the living room. A few minutes later, the wife, now stark naked, throws open the living room door and cries, "Come and get it!"

She's Having a Baby

A mother and father returned home early from a night out and found their 15-year-old daughter and her boyfriend naked, making love on the living room floor.

In a rage, the father dragged the boy outside, while the mother sat her daughter down on the couch for a talk.

"I'm not going to lecture you," the mother began. "Instead, I want to talk to you about taking precautions."

"Oh Mom. I know all about this stuff. I've been real careful.

In fact, I've been using your birth control pills."

The mother was silent for a moment. "Honey, why would you make up a story like that? None of my birth control pills have been missing. I think we better make an appointment with the doctor in the morning."

The girl sighed heavily. "I'm not making up a story. I *have* been using your birth control pills. You haven't noticed because I've been replacing the ones I took with aspirin."

The next morning, the mother made an appointment with her doctor. He told her she was pregnant.

The Stuck Couple

Two policemen were cruising the block when they heard the long blare of a car horn. Following the sound to its source, they found a man and a woman trapped inside a brand-new Ferrari, completely naked in the missionary position. In the tiny confines of the car, the man had thrown his back out and they had been unable to free themselves from their loving embrace.

Unfortunately, the policemen couldn't untangle the couple either.

"Look folks," said one police officer. "We're going to get an ambulance out here and a wrecking crew."

"Oh no!" cried the woman.

"Do it!" the man said. "Do anything you can to get us out of here."

Once the wrecking crew arrived, they saw only one way to free the lovers. They sawed the roof off the Ferrari. Then the paramedics lifted the man out of the car and onto a stretcher.

Before they left for the hospital, one of the paramedics came up to the woman and said, "Don't worry ma'am. It's just a slipped disc."

"I don't care about him!" she exclaimed. "What I'm worried about is how I'm going to explain to my husband what happened to his car!"

Variations: In one telling of the story, the lovers decide to go at it while parked outside the woman's house. Another bizarre version insists that if a woman is startled while making love, her muscles cramp, making it impossible for the man to withdraw.

The Surprise Lover

Two high school sweethearts from Long Beach Island on the Jersey shore pitched a small tent behind some sand dunes so that they could spend the night together.

About an hour later, two police officers spotted the tent on the beach. The first cop lifted the flap, looked inside and said, "You kids are in big trouble."

"Please officer," said the boy, "give us a break."

"Kid," said the cop, "fornicating in public is a serious offense in this town."

That's when the girl spoke up. "Maybe we can come to an understanding, officer. If I make love to you and your partner, will you let us go?"

"No!" cried the boy.

"Sure!" said the cop.

"Eddie," said the girl, "this way our parents will never know. Now step outside."

Poor Eddie couldn't stand it, so he ran down the beach while the first officer entered the tent.

After a time, the officer crawled out. "Your turn," he said to his partner.

The second cop turned on his flashlight and crawled into the tent.

"Oh no!" he cried.

The girl shrieked, "Daddy!"

Variation: In another version, a father visits his daughter at her college. Back at his hotel, he feels restive and calls an escort service to send someone over to spend the night with him. The prostitute who comes to his hotel room is his own daughter.

The Unseemly Stain

A young woman's parents were going away for the weekend, so she invited her fiancé over. "We have the whole weekend," she told him. "We'll make love in every room in the house."

On Friday night, they started their marathon in the living room—on the parents' brand new white couch. When they got up the next morning, they discovered an unseemly stain on the white upholstery.

"Don't worry," the fiancé said. "I'll get some furniture cleaner. The stain will come right out."

But furniture cleaner didn't work. Neither did the more abrasive stain removers. Not even straight bleach eliminated the stain.

"We're screwed," the guy said.

"Not necessarily," the woman said. "All we have to do is put the blame on somebody else. Get your car keys."

On Sunday afternoon, when the parents returned home, the couple met them the front door with a welcome-home gift—an adorable golden retriever puppy.

A Night with Batman

A woman on a business trip was sitting in a hotel bar in Dallas when she was approached by a very handsome man. Usually she rebuffed strangers, but this guy was too good to resist. She let him buy her a drink, and then another. And then another. After a couple of hours of conversation, the man invited the woman upstairs to his hotel room.

Once they were alone, the man asked her, "Are you playful?"

"I'm ready for anything," the woman said.

So the man undressed her and laid her down on the bed. From the nightstand drawer he pulled out four white silk ropes and tied the woman's wrists and ankles to the bedposts.

"I'll be back in a moment," he said, and went into the bathroom.

A few minutes later, he bounded back into the room dressed in a Batman costume, crying, "Don't worry, miss! I'll save you!"

After striking a heroic pose, the man leapt onto the dresser. But he lost his footing, slipped, hit his head and knocked himself cold.

The woman tugged at the silk ropes, but she couldn't get free. She waited for half an hour, but still "Batman" did not regain consciousness. Desperate, humiliated and cold, she began to scream for help.

Guests in the adjoining room heard her frantic cries and called the front desk. Within minutes, hotel security, the hotel manager and a small crowd of guests from nearby rooms burst through the door.

"I'm getting real tired of this," said the hotel security officer as he untied the woman. "Tell your friend Batman that the next time he comes to Dallas, I'd like him to stay at a different hotel."

Variations: The most common alternate version of this story features a married couple. The husband ties his wife to the bed, puts on a Superman costume and knocks himself unconscious while leaping from tall furniture in a single bound. In another variant, the victim is a traveling businessman and the would-be superhero is a transvestite.

The Costume Party

A married couple was invited to their friends' annual Halloween costume party. The husband announced that he would go as Zorro, but the wife insisted upon keeping her costume a secret. On the day of the party, the wife fell ill. "You go anyway," she told her husband. "I'll be fine here."

Reluctantly, the husband put on his Zorro costume and went off to the party.

A couple of hours later, the woman felt much better, so she decided she would go to the party after all. And since her husband did not know that she was coming dressed as a French maid, it would give her an opportunity to see how her husband acted when she was not around.

The party was in full swing when the wife arrived. The wife

spotted Zorro right away—he was dancing with a buxom milkmaid. Then he had a couple of drinks with a sexy female vampire. Afterwards, he returned to the dance floor with a leggy blonde dressed in a parochial schoolgirl uniform.

When the dance was over, the wife decided to test her husband's fidelity. She sidled up to Zorro and said, "Could you get a lady a drink?"

After a little chatter at the bar, they headed out to the dance floor. She whispered in his ear, "I don't suppose they have any empty bedrooms around here."

"I know they do," Zorro said. "Let's go."

Hand-in-hand, they hurried upstairs and slipped into an empty bedroom. "Keep the lights off and your mask on," the wife said.

"Anything you say," Zorro answered.

After they made love, the woman kissed her masked lover and wished him goodnight. Then she hurried home, hid her costume in the back of the closet and climbed into bed.

About an hour later, her husband returned.

"How was the party?" she asked.

"Not so great," the husband replied. "I really don't have much fun without you."

"You're so sweet. So what did you do all this time? It's after one in the morning. That's a long time to be miserable at a party."

"Oh, I spent the night in the hot tub. One of the guests came to the party without a costume, so I loaned him my Zorro outfit. He told me he had a terrific time tonight."

The Unzipped Fly

A woman came home from the grocery store and saw her husband working under the car. She was in a playful mood, so as she passed she reached down, unzipped his fly and fondled him for a moment. Then she went into the house.

There was her husband, sprawled on the couch in front of the television, watching a football game.

"What are you doing here?" she exclaimed.

The husband looked confused. "I'm watching the game."

"Then who's that under the car?"

"That's Neal. Our mechanic."

"Oh no. You're not going to believe what I just did. I thought it was you, so I pulled down his zipper and played with him a little. If you get my drift."

"Neal's gonna love this," said the husband. "Come on, I'll go with you and help explain."

They found Neal, still under the car, out cold. When the lady of the house had unzipped him, he was so startled that he tried to sit up and knocked himself out on the muffler.

The Erotic Video Scam

A scam artist placed small ads in Australian newspapers and magazines advertising a series of erotic videos at very reasonable prices. Soon the orders began to pour in. In an average week, the scam artist was depositing $10,000 in checks from his buyers.

But none of the customers ever received any videos. Instead, they got an apologetic letter from the company saying that it was unable to fulfill their order. "We are deeply sorry for any disappointment," the letter read, "and we are pleased to enclose a refund."

Printed in large black type across the top of the refund checks was the company name: "Bestiality and Other Perversions Video."

Few of the customers could bring themselves to present the check to their banks. The scam artist made off with over $200,000.

Artificially Endowed

Inspired by the movie *Saturday Night Fever*, a kid from the Bensonhurst neighborhood in Brooklyn started hanging out at discos. After a few nights at the clubs, he realized that women were less interested in men who were good dancers (he happened to be pretty good on the dance floor) than with men whose tight pants revealed an entirely different kind of endowment.

So the following Saturday he put on a tight pair of black polyester pants, and then squeezed a thick 8-inch-long plastic tube into the crotch. It pressed uncomfortably against the inside of his thigh. In fact, it hurt. But when he looked in the full-length mirror he smiled at what he saw. Tonight he would be irresistible.

The kid was a big hit with the women at the disco. His only problem was which one he would go home with that night. Then around midnight, while he was on the dance floor, he felt lightheaded and couldn't keep his balance. The lights and the crowd began to whirl around him. A moment later, he collapsed.

When the kid woke up in the emergency room, he was wearing a hospital gown. A nurse stood beside his bed. In her hand was the 8-inch plastic tube.

"What happened?" the kid asked. "What's wrong with me?"

"It's your plastic friend here," the nurse said. "It pressed up against the arteries in your crotch and cut off the circulation. That's why you passed out."

She tossed the tube into his lap. "You can go home now. You'll be fine. But just a little advice: next time, stuff your pants with tissues."

The Turkey Neck

On New Year's Day in Scotland, a newly married man went out drinking with two of his buddies. By the time the pub closed, they were all staggering drunk, but the young husband was in worse shape than his two friends.

His friends carried him home, fished his house keys out of his pocket and carried him into the parlor where they laid him down on the carpet.

"I'm feeling a bit hungry," said one. "How about you?"

"A snack would be good right about now," said the other. "Let's go into the kitchen and see if we can find the remains of the missus's New Year's turkey."

They hauled the leftover turkey out of the fridge and carved themselves generous slices. When they were ready to go, the first friend said, "I have an idea."

He took the turkey neck into the parlor where the man of the house was still passed out on the carpet. The friend unzipped the husband's fly and let the turkey neck dangle out. Snorting with suppressed laughter, the two drunks slipped out of the house as quietly as they could.

Very early the next morning, the wife woke up. When she realized she was in bed alone, she put on her robe and went downstairs. There was her husband, asleep on the carpet. Crouched between his legs was the family's cat, eating what the wife took to be her husband's penis. "No!" she screamed. At which point the cat took fright, seized the turkey neck and ran. The woman fainted from the shock, but the commotion woke her husband, who found his fly open, his wife collapsed at the foot of the stairs and his cat running around with a turkey neck.

Variation: An alternate version is also told in Scotland, in which the drunk's friends take him home and the wife makes a bed for him on the sofa. Before they leave, the two pals unzip their friend's fly and slip in the turkey neck—all unbeknownst to the wife. During the night, she goes down to see how her husband is faring and finds the cat chewing on the turkey neck. She faints from the shock and breaks her arm.

The Honeymooners

A newlywed couple spent their honeymoon at a theme hotel that featured giant round beds, mirrored walls, large whirlpool baths and complimentary champagne. It was tacky, but the couple got into the spirit of the place and had some of the best sex of their lives.

Their first anniversary rolled around and they decided to go back to the hotel for a romantic weekend.

When they checked into their suite, they found that everything was exactly as they had remembered it—with one exception. Now there was a large screen TV with a VCR and a library of adult videos.

"What do you say we uncork this champagne and watch a

video?" said the husband.

"Fine with me," said the wife. "You pick something while I change."

"They've got a movie called *The Honeymooners*," the husband called to his wife.

"Sounds perfect," she answered from the bathroom.

A moment later, the wife emerged from the bathroom in a lacy red-and-black teddy. The husband had stripped down to his red silk boxers. He popped in the video, and the couple settled back into a mountain of pillows covered in red velour.

"Look," said the husband, "the set looks just like this room."

"And the guy is wearing a leather jockstrap, just like the one I gave you for our honeymoon," said the wife.

As the camera moved in for a close up, the wife let out a shrill scream. "That *is* you. And that's *me* on the bed!"

Caught in the Pumpkin Patch

Police in Westchester County, New York, arrested a 27-year-old man in a pumpkin patch at 11:38 PM on a Saturday toward the end of October. The charges were lewd and lascivious behavior, public indecency and driving while intoxicated.

In court, the man said that he had gone out to a bar for a few beers and some company. Getting the beers was no trouble. But finding a woman who would go home with him wasn't nearly as easy.

"About eleven-thirty, I was pretty frustrated, so I decided to go home," the man testified. "I was feeling the need real bad when I passed this pumpkin patch. It occurred to me that pumpkins are nice and soft inside. So I pulled over. There was nobody around for miles. Or at least I thought nobody was around.

"I picked out a nice pumpkin, cut a hole in it with my pocket knife and let nature follow its course."

The arresting officer testified that when she approached the man she said, "'Excuse me sir, but do you realize you are screwing a pumpkin?' Then he answered, 'A pumpkin! Damn, is it midnight already?'"

He was found guilty on all charges.

Walking the Dog

Every evening after dinner, a husband took his Labrador retriever on a four-mile walk. One day he came down with a bad case of the flu, so it fell to his wife to walk the dog.

After supper, she clipped on the dog's leash, and they headed out the door. She wanted to go to a large open lot at the end of the street, but the dog tugged at the leash and all but dragged her around the block to a house on the corner. The dog pulled the poor woman up the stairs and began scratching furiously at the door.

The wife scolded the dog and was trying to pull it away when she heard a sweet female voice inside the house call, "You're a little early today, darling! Just one minute."

The next moment, the door swung wide open and there stood a pretty young woman in a sexy negligee holding a large bone in her hand. "This should keep the dog happy while we're—Uh-oh."

The Bad Bachelorette

The friends of a future bride arranged a raucous bachelorette party for her, including live entertainment provided by a male stripper, a handsome black bodybuilder.

By the time he arrived, the bride had had one drink too many. After the show, she took the stripper by the hand and led him to a bedroom for a private performance.

The stripper left a couple of hours later, and the bride woke up the next morning with no memory of the night's events. Her friends had already decided among themselves to keep the story a secret, so the wedding went on as planned.

When the newlyweds returned from their honeymoon, the wife discovered that she was pregnant. The happy couple waited eagerly for their first child. Nine months later, the woman went into labor. The husband was at her side in the delivery room. "Here we go," said the doctor. "It's a . . ." And then he stopped.

"What's the matter, Doc?" said the husband. "Can't you tell if it's a boy or a girl?"

Without a word, the doctor held up a healthy little mixed-race boy.

Variations: In another version of the story, the woman gives birth to twins: one white, one black. In some retellings of the legend, the husband storms out of the delivery room and files for divorce.

The Clogged Toilet

The toilet in a couple's master bedroom kept backing up. The husband tried the plunger and poured drain opener down by the quart, but nothing worked. Finally, he called a plumber.

In a matter of minutes, the plumber found the obstruction. He pulled up a mass of condoms—dozens of them—that had lodged in the line.

"Look mister," the plumber said, "I'm really happy for you that you've got such an active love life. But just toss these babies in the garbage and you won't clog up your toilet anymore. Okay?"

The husband was quiet for a moment. He didn't use condoms. But he wasn't going to tell the plumber that. "Right. Thanks for the advice."

After the plumber left, the husband confronted his wife with the wad of condoms. "Anybody I know?" he asked.

"No. You don't know him. He's the landscaper. He shows up after you've left for work."

The next day, the husband left for work at the usual time. But instead of going to the office, he hid in the woods across the street from his house. He had his shotgun with him. Around ten o'clock, the landscaper pulled his truck into the driveway. As he stepped out of the cab, the husband fired.

The landscaper fell to the ground with his backside full of birdshot. The wife hurried from the house. "You idiot!" she screamed. "My boyfriend is on vacation. This guy is just covering for him!"

The Baby Train

The census bureau in Canberra, Australia, was surprised to learn that in a little oceanfront town north of Sydney the birthrate was three times the national average. One employee at the bureau was so intrigued that he made a special trip to the town to learn more about it.

When he arrived he saw kids everywhere. All the schools were jammed. The maternity section was the largest wing of the local hospital. Every park and playground was swarming with kids.

Aside from the extraordinary number of children, the town

seemed like any other place in Australia. Nor could the census bureau employee detect anything special about the adults. So he stopped by the town hall to see if he could learn anything there.

The mayor welcomed him into his office.

"Mayor, I couldn't help noticing all the children around here."

"Yes, we are especially blessed with little ones. My wife and I have eight, you know."

"Congratulations," the census bureau employee replied. "If you could throw any light on your town's high birthrate, the census bureau would appreciate it."

"It's very simple. It has to do with the *Kyogle Mail.*"

"That's a train, isn't it?" the visitor from Canberra said.

"Absolutely."

"A train is the reason your town's birthrate is three times the national average?"

"Yes. Let me explain. The railway line makes an S-curve through our town. When the train crosses the town line, about four-thirty every morning, it blows its whistle which wakes up everybody in the place. Two miles later, when it's on its way out of town, it blows the whistle again. Well, it's too early to get up, but hardly worth falling back to sleep. So to fill the time before the alarm clock goes off . . . ."

Variations: Many places claim that an early morning train gives their town or region an unusually high birthrate—from the campus of Michigan State University to small towns in rural Utah.

The Stylist Makes a Mistake

An unkempt man walked into a styling salon in a shopping mall about half an hour before closing and asked for a haircut. The man looked strange, and the stylist was hesitant because she was working alone and there were no other customers around. But in the end she agreed to give him a haircut.

She pinned the sheet around his neck and had just picked up her comb and scissors when she noticed the man's hand moving up and down in his lap beneath the sheet. Thinking he was a sexual deviant with a hair fetish, she hit him with a large bottle of shampoo and knocked the man out cold. Then she called the mall's security department.

When security arrived, the man was still unconscious and the stylist was standing over him, holding her shampoo bottle. When the police removed the sheet, they saw the man's hands in his lap, holding a handkerchief and a pair of eyeglasses.

Variations: In English versions of this legend, the hairdresser knocks the man out with a hairdryer. There is another English version in which the stylist grabs a large hair brush and hits the lump under the sheet, breaking the man's glasses.

"Go For It, Mr. Gorsky"

As astronaut Neil Armstrong took his first step on the moon, he uttered those immortal words, "One small step for man, one giant leap for mankind." A moment later, mission control heard Armstrong say, "Go for it, Mr. Gorsky."

Nobody at NASA had any idea what Armstrong was talking about. At first some thought that it was a private message to a fellow astronaut, but there was no one named Gorsky in the American or in the Soviet space program. Once he was back on earth, Armstrong brushed off all inquiries saying it must have been a jumbled transmission.

Twenty-six years later, Armstrong and a friend from NASA were having dinner together. As they reminisced about the old days, the friend asked Armstrong, "So what was that 'Go for it, Mr. Gorsky' remark all about?"

Armstrong sighed and said, "Well, he's passed on now, so I suppose I can tell you the story. Years ago, when I was in high school, I was playing baseball with my brother. He hit a foul ball that flew over the fence and into our neighbors' bushes. Our neighbors were the Gorskys. It was summer and all the windows were open. So when

I went into the bushes to get the ball, I heard Mrs. Gorsky say, "You want to know when I'll give you oral sex? I'll tell you when. I'll give you oral sex when the kid next door walks on the moon!"

THE STOLEN KIDNEY AND OTHER MEDICAL MISHAPS

THE STOLEN KIDNEY AND OTHER MEDICAL MISHAPS

The Stolen Kidney

A business traveler from New York was sitting in the bar of his hotel in Rio de Janeiro when two well-dressed men took the seats beside him. While the two men waited for their drinks, they struck up a conversation with the American. They introduced themselves as executives at the Bank of Brazil. Soon, all three were deep in discussion about international trade. After a couple of drinks at the bar, the three men had dinner together in the restaurant. Then they returned to the bar for a few more drinks.

Some hours later, the American traveler awoke in the bathtub of his hotel room, naked and submerged up to his neck in ice. Scrawled in large letters on the wall facing him was the message, "Don't move. Just call 911." On a small table beside the bathtub was a telephone.

When the 911 operator picked up the man said, "I don't know what's happened to me. My back hurts. I'm in a bathtub filled with ice and there's this message that I must not move until I've called 911. But I don't know what the emergency might be."

"Sir," the operator said, "it is important that you remain calm. I've received calls like this before. Now, reach behind you carefully.

Can you feel a tube in your lower back?"

The man did as he was instructed.

"Yes. There's a tube back there. What does it mean?"

"Sir, please keep still. I've already traced your call and sent an ambulance to your hotel. They'll be there soon."

In a few minutes, the man heard the door to his room open. "I'm in the bathroom," he cried.

A team of paramedics, hotel security and the hotel manager filled the room. They lifted him carefully onto a gurney and rushed him to the nearest emergency room.

"What's wrong with me?" the man asked.

"The doctors at the hospital must examine you first," the paramedics told him.

In the emergency room, a doctor performed a quick examination. "It's as we suspected," he said. "Sir, I am afraid that whoever you were with this evening drugged you and harvested one of your kidneys while you were unconscious."

"One of my kidneys is gone?!"

"Yes sir," the doctor replied. "But you are fortunate. I have seen cases where the thieves took both."

Variations: In some tellings of this legend, the unsuspecting donor is seduced by a beautiful stranger who takes him back to her hotel room where, after making love, the victim is drugged and a surgical SWAT team harvests his kidney. The version told in Central and South America is even more gruesome: Babies are kidnapped and murdered for their organs.

The Unsuspecting Donor

Mike, a salesman from Philadelphia, was driving one Monday night in winter when his car hit a patch of black ice and slammed sideways into a tree. When the paramedics arrived, they found him unconscious and his right leg severed just below the knee. They packed the limb in ice and rushed Mike and his leg to the hospital, but the damage to his knee was too extensive for the doctors to reattach the leg. He would have to be fitted with a prosthetic device.

Mike took the bad news well—he had lost a leg, but at least he was still alive. And he was eager to begin physical therapy so he could become accustomed to his prosthetic leg.

Two weeks later, at a therapy session, Mike met a guy named Ray who worked construction. Ray's right foot had been crushed in an accident on the job and the doctors had been forced to amputate.

"But I was lucky," Ray told Mike, "because the hospital found a donor and the doctor attached that foot to my leg. I've got some feeling back already and I can even bend a couple of my toes. The only trouble is my left foot is a size eight, while my new foot is a size ten. Learning how to walk again is tough enough without having feet that don't match."

Mike was quiet for a minute.

"When did they give you your new foot?" Mike asked.

"Two weeks ago. On a Monday night."

"And the docs said that a donor came in that evening?"

"Right."

"Does your new foot have a mole on the big toe?"

"Yeah, it does. Hey, why all the questions?"

"Because," said Mike, "that's my foot you're wearing."

The Stomach Pump Luncheon

Although this story appears in John Berendt's recent bestseller Midnight in the Garden of Good and Evil, *the origins of the legend go back at least to the 1940s.*

During the week between Christmas and New Year's, a prominent Los Angeles socialite hosted a holiday luncheon. For the fish course she served generous portions of a delicious salmon mousse.

While the maid served the salad, the hostess went into the kitchen to see how the rest of the meal was coming along. She found her cat on the kitchen counter, gobbling up the remainder of the salmon mousse. The hostess grabbed the cat, opened the back door and tossed it outside. Then she returned to her guests.

The rest of the meal went off without a hitch, and the hostess knew that her party was a triumph. But while her guests were lingering over their coffee and dessert, the maid approached and whispered in the hostess's ear, "Ma'am, could I speak with you for a moment, please? There's been a bit of trouble."

The hostess excused herself and went into the kitchen with the maid. There, lying on the kitchen floor, was the hostess's cat. It was dead.

"I found him this way by the curb," the maid said. "I don't know what happened."

"Oh no!" said the hostess. "I caught him eating the salmon mousse. He must have died of ptomaine! What will I tell my guests?"

She rushed back to the dining room, where she made an announcement. "My dear friends, I regret to say that it has just come to my attention that the salmon mousse was a bit off. As a precaution, it would be best if we all went to the Mercy Hospital emergency room."

At the hospital, the emergency room doctors insisted that the hostess and her guests have their stomachs pumped. It was a horrible ordeal for everyone.

That evening, the hostess was in her sitting room, trying to recover from the humiliation of having nearly poisoned all of her friends. The doorbell rang and rather than wait for the maid, she answered it herself. A neighbor from down the street stood on the doorstep.

"Dorothy," he said, "my conscience has been bothering me all day. So don't say a word, just hear me out. This afternoon, about lunchtime, I hit your cat with my car. I couldn't bring myself to tell you, so I just left its body by the curb. Can you forgive me?"

The Backwards, Bare-Bottomed Skier

A young woman went with several friends for a ski weekend in Aspen. Although she was still fairly inexperienced, her friends talked her into joining them on one of the more challenging slopes.

There was a long line at the chairlift and while she waited the woman felt the need to use the ladies' room. "Don't worry," one of her friends told her. "There are probably restrooms at the top."

It was another 20 minutes before the young woman finally got a chair and the long ride, especially in subfreezing weather, only added to her discomfort. By the time the chair arrived at the top of the slope, the need was urgent. And then she discovered that there were no restrooms.

"I'll have to go in the woods," she told her friends. "Keep your fingers crossed that nobody sees me."

She found some rhododendron bushes that looked like they

would give her cover. With a sigh of relief, the young woman scrambled behind the bushes. She was just about done when she felt herself beginning to slide. She grabbed a branch, but it snapped in her hand. Suddenly she was skiing swiftly down the hill, backwards, with her ski pants around her ankles and her bare bottom completely exposed. She shot down the slope in a straight line, picking up momentum, until she crashed into a pylon.

The ski patrol arrived a few minutes later, pulled up her pants, put a splint on her broken arm and rushed her to a hospital emergency room.

As she was resting in bed, waiting for her friends to come and pick her up, a hospital orderly wheeled another bed into the room. It was a young man with a broken leg.

To pass the time she asked, "Did you break that on the slopes?"

"Oh yeah," he answered. "And in the damnedest way possible. I had just started my run, when out of the bushes comes this woman skiing backwards, with her pants around her ankles. I couldn't take my eyes off her. That's when I skied right into a tree. So what happened to you?"

The woman hesitated for a moment. "I slipped climbing out of the bathtub."

Variations: This story varies only in its setting. It is usually set in

Vail or Aspen, but many people have heard it from "a friend of a friend" who "really saw it" while skiing in Pennsylvania or Canada. In Sweden this story was reported on the evening news as an actual event.

The Infected Needle in the Pay Phone

A young woman stopped to use a pay phone in New York City's East Village. When she completed her call, she stuck her index finger into the coin return slot to check if a previous caller had left some change behind. But instead of finding a coin, she felt a sharp pain in her finger.

She yanked her finger out. It was bleeding. She looked inside the coin return and saw a hypodermic needle jammed inside. "Damn New Yorkers," she said. "I hate this town."

She wiped off the blood with a tissue and went about her business.

A couple of weeks later, the young woman felt ill and went to her doctor. As part of the examination, her doctor drew some blood and sent it to the lab. "I'll call you with the results tomorrow," he said.

First thing the next morning, the young woman got a call from her doctor asking her to come by his office so they could review the test results.

He invited her into his private office and closed the door. As he sat down in the chair beside her, he said, "I'll have to ask you some personal questions. Do you practice safe sex?"

"Of course. Why do you ask?"

"Have you ever been an intravenous drug user?"

"No! Never! What are you saying?"

"Just one last question. Have you used a pay phone lately?"

"Yes. A couple of weeks ago. I remember because someone had put a needle in the coin slot and I pricked my finger on it when I checked for change."

The doctor was silent for a moment.

"We've learned recently that some drug users are disposing of their used needles in pay phones. Most likely their motive is revenge for becoming infected with hepatitis or some other disease."

"Are you telling me that needle gave me hepatitis?"

"No," the doctor said. "I'm afraid that needle infected you with HIV."

Variations: In a popular alternate version of this legend, the victim feels a pinprick when he or she takes a seat in a movie theater. Another less common variant has the victim being pricked in a crowded place, such as on a bus or a subway.

The Oozing Brain

The invention of slice-and-bake cookie dough gave birth to this legend.

A woman in Baltimore belonged to a volunteer organization that ran errands for invalids and the elderly. During an August heatwave, she received a call from an elderly woman who needed someone to do a little grocery shopping for her. The elderly woman read off her shopping list and then gave her address. It was a rundown part of the inner city, but the volunteer couldn't refuse the poor woman.

The volunteer drove to the supermarket, picked up everything the elderly woman had asked for and then headed for the rough part of town. It was as bad as she suspected: burnt-out buildings, vacant lots strewn with garbage, groups of hoodlums gathered on every corner. The volunteer was so frightened that she locked her doors and rolled up all the windows. Her car was not air-conditioned and within minutes it was a sweltering oven.

Then the woman heard a loud "Pop!" and felt something oozing down the back of her neck.

"My God!" she cried. "I've been shot!"

Somehow, she regained her composure and drove to a nearby hospital. Through superhuman effort, she even walked into the emergency room where she told the nurses at the desk that she had been shot in the head. Immediately, a team of doctors and nurses put her on an operating table and rolled her into an examining room.

"Where's the wound?" one doctor said. "I can't see any blood."

"Look at the back of my head!" the woman cried. "Can't you see my brains oozing out?"

Carefully, the doctor turned the woman's head. He touched the wet, white mass that clung to her hair.

"Ma'am," the doctor said, "this isn't your brain. It's slice-and-bake cookie dough."

The Menopausal Party Girl

A mother in the throes of menopause decided to visit her daughter in San Francisco. After a couple of days, the mother was so cranky and physically uncomfortable that the daughter implored her to visit her gynecologist. Under the best of circumstances, the mother did not like going to a gynecologist, let alone a strange one in a strange city. But her daughter assured her that this one was considerate and kind and had a charming sense of humor. At last the mother agreed to go.

On the morning of her appointment, the mother was very nervous. She took a bath. Then she took a shower. She used deodorant from head to toe and even borrowed her daughter's vaginal spray. Ready at last, she called a cab to take her to the doctor's office.

The gynecologist was everything her daughter said he would be. Thoughtful, gentle and very sweet. But when he began his examination, he said, "Well, it looks like we've got a party girl here!"

"What did you say to me?"

"I said that you must be quite the party girl." Then the gynecologist smirked and winked at the woman.

Completely humiliated, the woman did not utter another word for the remainder of the examination. When it was over, she dressed quickly and hurried out of the office.

That night the daughter came home from work and found her mother in tears.

"What happened? What did the doctor tell you?"

"He took one look down there and he called me a party girl," the mother wailed.

"He said what?!"

"He said I was a party girl. I've never been so humiliated in my life."

"I don't understand. It's not like him at all. Let's take a deep breath and go over this slowly. What did you do before you left the house for your appointment?"

"Well, I was extremely careful about hygiene. I took a bath and a shower—just to be on the safe side. I used plenty of deodorant. And I borrowed your vaginal spray."

"Mother, I don't have any vaginal spray."

"Of course you do. I'll show you."

Together, they walked to the bathroom where the mother pulled the spray bottle from the cupboard beneath the sink.

"Oh Mom!" the daughter cried. "That's not vaginal spray. That's the gold glitter hairspray I used last year at Halloween."

The Contaminated Tampon

Several years ago a new tampon was introduced on the market. It was attractively packaged and reasonably priced, so many women tried the new product. But over time, many of the women who used the new tampon noticed that their periods were heavier than they had been before. Some women sent letters urging a consumer advocacy group to investigate the product.

In their labs, the advocacy group found that the tampon included asbestos. Asbestos induces bleeding. Naturally, if a woman's flow is heavier, she will have buy more tampons.

The advocacy group published their results in a woman's magazine, and the manufacturer was forced to take their tampons off the market.

AIDS Mary

A woman from Seattle named Mary decided to escape the rainy

winter months and spend a few weeks in Aruba. Her travel agent booked her a suite in a deluxe resort hotel on a gorgeous private beach. Thirty minutes after she checked in, Mary was lounging on the beach enjoying the attentions of a very handsome cabana boy.

The cabana boy set up a large beach umbrella for her, brought her fresh towels and refreshing drinks from the bar and even rubbed sunscreen on her back and shoulders. Mary relished the luxury of having a personal attendant.

Then one evening, as she was about to go to bed, there was a knock at her door. It was the cabana boy with a bottle of Dom Perignon and a bowl of strawberries. Mary invited him in and they spent the night together. In fact, they spent every night of Mary's vacation together.

On the morning of her departure, Mary almost wept at the thought of leaving her handsome young lover. After they had said their good-byes, a woman from the front desk took Mary aside.

"Excuse my intrusion, miss," she said. "But have you been intimate with that man?"

"How dare you stick your nose in my business! Where's the hotel manager?" Mary exclaimed.

"I know I have offended you, miss. Do whatever you must. But take my advice as well: When you return home, go to your doctor and have a blood test. That boy has AIDS and he does not care if he infects anyone else."

Mary was shocked and terrified. Back in Seattle, her doctor gave her the bad news: She was indeed infected with HIV.

Mary spent days locked in her apartment weeping. But then she became angry. Since the boy in Aruba was doing all he could to infect unsuspecting women, she would seduce every man she could.

That night Mary went to a hotel bar and picked up a business-man. The next morning, when the man woke up, he found that Mary was gone. But in the bathroom, scrawled across the mirror in blood-red lipstick was the message, "Welcome to the world of AIDS!"

Variations: One version of the story presents AIDS Mary as espe-cially vindictive: She dates each of her victims for at least a month to increase her chance of infecting them with HIV. In some tellings, Mary is a prostitute who is retaliating for her mistreatment at the hands of men. Another variant is about AIDS John, a bisexual Ameri-can soldier who infects both men and women.

The Orgasmic Side-Effect

A clinical psychiatrist in Canada discovered an unusual side effect to a new antidepressant drug.

One day, a male patient who was taking the antidepressant called. "Doc, this stuff is great!" he said. "I want to stay on it for life."

The psychiatrist said that if his depression was in complete remission, then they should suspend the treatment.

"No way, doc," said the patient. "Since I've started taking these little pills, every time I yawn I have an incredible orgasm. Of course, it's a little embarrassing ejaculating in the office or on the train. But I'm willing to put up with the inconvenience—this is the best antidepressant I've ever had!"

The Hairball

In the middle of math class, a fourth-grade girl clutched her stomach, let out a sharp scream and fell to the floor. By the time her teacher reached her, the child was dead.

The rest of the students became hysterical. The principal closed the school for the rest of the day and called the parents, the police and an emergency medical team.

"I don't know what happened," the teacher said, sobbing. "She was working quietly on the math problems I had assigned, and chewing on the ends of her braids like she always did when she was concentrating hard. Then she cried out and fell out of her chair."

The police and the medical team held a brief conference together and then announced to the parents, "We're awfully sorry to do this to you folks. But we'll have to perform an autopsy."

The next day, the parents met with the county coroner. "I

understand your daughter was in the habit of chewing on her braids whenever she was doing her schoolwork."

"That's right," the father said. "All her teachers said the harder she was working, the harder she'd chew on her braids. It was so sweet."

The coroner shuffled some papers on his desk top and cleared his throat several times.

"We found that your daughter died of a large obstruction in her intestine. You see, she wasn't merely chewing on her hair. She was eating it. It formed a hairball in her stomach. And it was the hairball that killed her."

Variations: The most common variant of this legend is of a barber who keels over at work one day. An autopsy reveals that he was suffocated by an enormous hairball in his esophagus, the result of years of breathing in his clients' hair.

The Lost and Found False Teeth

Three men, all of them about 65, went deep-sea fishing off the coast of South Africa. They hadn't been out long when one of the three became violently seasick. Worse, as he vomited over the side he lost his set of false teeth.

Nauseous, angry and depressed, the frustrated fisherman went off by himself into the ship's cabin.

Not long afterwards, one of the fishermen hooked a swordfish. They called to their friend to come out and share the excitement of the catch, but he wasn't interested.

"Let's try to cheer him up a bit," the guy who caught the fish said. With that, he removed his own set of false teeth and put them in the swordfish's mouth. Then he called to his friend, "Charlie! Come here! You'll never believe it. This fish has got your teeth in its mouth!"

Charlie hurried out of the cabin. He opened the swordfish's mouth and pulled out the false teeth. "It's a miracle!" he said. "What are the chances of you boys catching the fish that swallowed my teeth?"

But as he inspected the set more closely, Charlie lost his enthusiasm. "I knew it was too good to be true," he said. "These teeth aren't mine."

And before his friends could say another word, Charlie tossed the false teeth over the side.

Sedating Rover

A veterinarian in a small Texas town hired a recent graduate from a veterinary college who was pleasant and eager, but had no experience with a practice. One day, while the vet had gone home to lunch, a man came in with an ancient, wheezing old mutt.

"I'm taking the whole family on a vacation to California," the man explained. "And it would be easier on Rover if you could put him to sleep."

The young vet-in-training scratched old Rover behind the ears, lifted him up on the examination table and gave him a lethal injection. In a few moments, Rover closed his eyes and passed quietly into eternity.

"Could you give me a hand getting the pooch in the back seat?" Rover's owner said.

As the young vet and the man wrestled Rover into the car, the man said, "Thanks for your help, Doc. Lord knows I love this dog. My kids are just nuts about him. But it's a long drive to California and as your boss can tell you, Rover really can't travel that far anymore without being sedated. See you when we come back!"

The young vet never said a word, just stood there and waved as the man drove off.

"If I'm lucky," he said to himself, "the family will think Rover passed away peacefully during the drive."

THE MURDERER IN THE
BACK SEAT AND OTHER
LEGENDS OF THE ROAD

THE MURDERER IN THE BACK SEAT AND OTHER LEGENDS OF THE ROAD

The Murderer in the Back Seat

A newspaper in Phoenix reported this legend as if it were a true story.
A woman walked out of a shopping mall near Phoenix, Arizona, and across the parking lot to her car. She was aware that a man was walking a few steps behind her, but she was not especially concerned: It was the middle of the afternoon and the lot was filled with people. She got to her car, climbed in, locked the doors and pulled out of the parking space. By coincidence, the man who had followed her was parked right next to her.

She drove to the exit. The man's car was directly behind her. She turned onto the highway. The man made the same turn. She accelerated, but the man kept up with her. In fact, now he was drawing closer, almost riding her rear bumper. And he began to flash his high beams.

Frightened now, she got off at an exit for downtown Phoenix. The man stayed with her. She sped through the city streets, running red lights in her panic. But she could not shake her pursuer.

So she headed toward the home of her brother-in-law, a police officer. Blaring her car horn, she pulled into the driveway. Her brother-in-law hurried out of his house.

"There's a man following me!" she cried. "All the way from the mall! There he is now!"

The stranger pulled his car into the driveway. The cop ran over shouting, "Phoenix Police! Get out of the car! What the hell do you think you're doing?"

As the stranger stepped out of his car, the cop wrestled him to the ground. "Take it easy, officer," he said. "I was just trying to warn the lady about the guy in the back seat of her car."

The cop stood up, pushed his sister-in-law away from the car and threw open the back door. There, huddled behind the driver's seat, was a man with a big hunting knife clutched in his hand.

Variations: In another version of the story, the woman pulls into a gas station late at night. When she hands over her credit card for payment, the attendant tells her that there is something wrong and convinces her to come into the office with him. He makes a phone call; moments later the police arrive and pull the would-be killer from the back seat.

The Hairy-Armed Hitchhiker

The earliest version of this legend dates from England, 1834.

A woman went to the supermarket late one rainy evening in the middle of the week. By the time she finished shopping, the store was about to close and the parking lot was almost empty. As she pushed her cart across the lot, a tall, heavy woman approached her.

"I'm so embarrassed," the strange woman said. "I came here to buy a few things, but once I got to the checkout counter, I found that I didn't have any money with me. Then I got outside just in time to see the tow truck taking away my car. It's been repossessed. I haven't been able to make the payments since I lost my job. Now it's raining and I don't have an umbrella and my apartment is five miles from here. This is so humiliating. Could you give me a ride home?"

The shopper hesitated for a moment. The stranger was definitely odd. Her clothes didn't fit very well, and her voice was harsh. But it was cold and the rain was coming down hard now.

"Yes. I can drive you home. It's no trouble at all."

The woman put her groceries in the trunk, then she and the stranger climbed into the car. As the stranger reached up for the seat belt, the sleeve of her coat slipped down. The woman saw a thick, hairy wrist. Like a man's.

Now she was frightened. What could she do to get this person out of her car?

They drove for a mile or two when she had an idea.

"Oh damn!" she said.

"Is something wrong?" the stranger asked.

"I think both of my tail-lights are out."

"Well, we aren't far from my place now. You can always take the car to the mechanic tomorrow."

"You don't understand. This happened once before and I was rear-ended. I spent three weeks in the hospital. I can't go through that again. Could you do me a favor? I'll pull over and you get out and see if at least one of the tail-lights is working. I'd feel so much better."

"Yeah. Sure," the stranger said.

So the woman pulled her car to the curb. "You're sweet to do this for me," she said.

Once the stranger had climbed out of the car, the woman hit the gas and sped away. She drove straight to the police station where she filed a report. "Now let's go outside and inspect your car," a police officer said.

Pointing to a large handbag on the front seat, the cop asked, "Is that yours, ma'am?"

"No. That's hers. Or his. It must have been left behind when I got her ... him ... to step out of the car."

"Let's see what we have here," the cop said. Pulling on a pair of latex gloves, he opened the bag. And drew out a large, sharp hatchet.

Variation: In the earliest printed version of this legend, a gentleman in a rig stops to give a lone woman a ride. Once he notices "her" hairy forearms, the hitchhiker runs off, leaving behind an overnight bag. Inside the gentleman finds a pair of loaded pistols.

The Headless Biker

On a road outside Newcastle, England, a man on a motorcycle drew up beside a large truck loaded with thin sheets of steel. Before the biker could pass the truck, the top sheet came loose, slid off the truck bed and neatly decapitated him.

Convulsively, the corpse tightened its grip on the hand throttle. The bike accelerated until it was even with the cab of the truck.

Glancing out his window, the truck driver saw the headless corpse riding a motorcycle. The horror of the sight gave him a heart attack. As the driver slumped over the wheel, the impact of his body turned the steering wheel slightly. The truck swerved to the right—and straight into a small crowd of people waiting for a bus, killing them instantly.

Variation: The most common alternate version of this story is of a beautiful collie who loves to ride in the family car with its head out the window. One day, a truck passes a little too closely to the car and the poor dog is decapitated.

The Snake in Her Jeans

On a warm summer's day in San Francisco, a woman headed out to her car to go shopping. As she backed her car out of the garage, she remembered that she had left her wallet in the house. Leaving the car door wide open, she went back inside. Five minutes later, with her wallet tucked in her purse, the woman pulled out of the driveway and headed for the city.

As she drove across the Golden Gate Bridge, she felt something tickling her ankle. She glanced down and saw a snake disappear up the leg of her jeans.

Screaming and kicking, she barely managed to pull her car to the side of the road. She leapt out of her car, shaking and slapping her leg until she fell to the ground shrieking.

A passing driver saw her and thought she was having an epileptic seizure. The woman was flailing about on the ground so wildly that the man was afraid she might hurt herself. He pulled over to help, but he was not a doctor and had no idea what to do. So he tried to hold her down.

Another driver saw what he took to be a woman struggling violently with an attacker on the side of the road. "I can't believe he's assaulting her in broad daylight!" he said to himself. He pulled over and grabbed the tire iron from his trunk. He took a good swing, caught the man along the side of his face and broke his jaw.

As the good Samaritan collapsed on the pavement, the woman's cries became even more hysterical. "It's not him!" she said. "It's the snake!"

The man with the tire iron was certain he had misunderstood the woman. But as he glanced down, he saw a small garter snake slither out from the leg of the woman's jeans.

Variations: In other versions of this legend, the woman is traveling with her pet mouse/gerbil/hamster in her lap. At some point during the drive, the little critter slips down to the floor of the car and climbs up the leg of the woman's pants.

"Pig!"

A man who was always self-conscious about his weight was speeding on a country road in Oregon one fine spring morning. At a fork in the road the driver bore to the left without reducing his speed. There was a farmer walking along the shoulder of the road. He looked up as the car approached and shouted at the driver, "Pig!"

The driver hung out the window of his car and shouted back, "You're not so great-looking yourself!"

Then he drew his head back into the car and returned his gaze to the road. As he rounded the next bend, he saw an enormous sow sunning herself in the middle of the road, only a couple of yards ahead of him.

The driver hit the brakes and tried to swerve around the animal. But the pig was too close and the car was moving too fast. All the driver heard was a squeal of terror and the brakes' screech as he plowed right into the pig.

The Flat Tire and the Madman

Late one night, a woman driving alone got a flat tire outside a hospital for the mentally unstable near Pendleton, Oregon. She was irritated that she would be delayed getting home and it was unnerving to be on a dark road alone late at night. But she knew how to change a flat; she could be on her way in 15 minutes.

She popped the trunk and took out the tire iron, the jack and the spare tire. She pried off the hubcap, removed the five lug nuts, and placed them inside the hubcap so she wouldn't lose them. As she reached for the jack, she heard a rustling sound in the bushes beside the fence. Looking over the rear fender of her car, she could see the dark, silent figure of a man pressed against the fence, watching her.

She tried to remain calm and keep her mind on her task. Her hands trembled slightly as she removed the flat tire and put on the spare. A high fence topped by coils of razor wire stood between her and the hospital patient who watched her, but she was still ill at ease. In her nervousness she kicked the hubcap. The woman's heart sank as she heard the lug nuts scatter into the tall grass along the side of the road. Frightened and frustrated, she began to cry.

"Don't cry," said the figure at the fence. "Don't cry. You can still fix the tire."

The woman stifled her sobs for a moment and listened.

"Take one lug nut from each of the other three tires. That will keep the spare on until you get home, or find a gas station."

The woman was still afraid, but she did as the stranger suggested. When the job was done, she managed to stammer out a "thank you."

"You're welcome," said the figure at the fence. As she drove away, the woman glanced back at the spot where the stranger had stood. But he had vanished.

The Severed Fingers

Versions of this legend date back to 16th-century France.

In the 1960s a college senior took his girlfriend to a drive-in movie in his new Volkswagen Beetle. Four loud, obnoxious guys in a beat-up Plymouth Valiant pulled into the space next to the young lovers. The guys hauled a case of beer out of the trunk, wedged it into the back seat of their car and settled back to watch the movie.

As the movie progressed, the four louts became drunker and drunker. They started a running commentary, in the foulest language, on the storyline of the movie and speculated on the sex lives of the actors.

The boy in the Volkswagen was getting angry. "I'll be right back," he told his girlfriend. Before she could stop him, he got out of his car and walked around to the drunks' car.

"You guys want to keep it down?" he said.

The loudmouths answered with a barrage of obscenities. The boyfriend answered in kind. As all four guys reached for the door handles, he realized that maybe a confrontation with a carload of drunks was not such a bright idea. He rushed back to the Volkswagen, rolled up the windows and locked the doors.

"We've got to go," he said to his girlfriend.

"I told you to leave them alone," she said, annoyed.

But no sooner had the ignition turned over than the four drunks surrounded the car. Three of them lifted the back of the car off the ground. Without any traction, the rear wheels spun helplessly in the air. The boyfriend kept gunning the engine.

"What are you doing?" his girlfriend screamed.

"They can't hold it up forever," the boyfriend said.

He was right. After a few minutes the exhaust fumes, combined with the weight of the car, became too much for the drunks. They dropped their load and the Volkswagen sped away.

"Did you hear a scream?" the girlfriend asked.

"No. And who cares if we did," he replied.

Back home, the boy inspected the rear of his Volkswagen for any sign of damage. As he rested his hand on the rear bumper, he felt something wet. Shining the flashlight at the spot, he first saw blood. Then he saw, wedged between the bumper and the trunk, three severed fingers.

Variations: The earliest printed version of this legend dates from a book published in France in 1579. A robber stops a horseman on a deserted road. To keep his victim from escaping, the highwayman wraps the horse's bridle around his fingers. Suddenly the rider uses his spurs and the horse bolts down the road, taking several of the bandit's fingers with him.

The Collision

One rainy evening in Germany, two trucks, coming from opposite directions, were speeding along a back road near Bonn. They both hit a slick stretch of road at the same time and plowed head-on into each other.

When the ambulance crew arrived they found that both drivers were dead. Meanwhile, the wrecking crew discovered that the impact of the collision had been so great that the trucks could not be pried apart. The trucks were towed to the junkyard as a single vehicle.

For the first day or so the wrecked trucks were a popular curiosity at the junkyard. Mechanics, used-car dealers and members of the highway patrol dropped by to inspect them. By the third day, however, the visitors were complaining of a foul smell.

"Something dead is in there," one of the highway cops told the foreman of the yard. "You better get it out before it becomes a health hazard."

"The ambulance pulled the bodies of the drivers from the wreck," the foreman answered. "What else could be in there?"

"The only way to find out," the cop told him, "is to pry those trucks apart."

The yard crew hooked up four huge tow trucks. To the screeching sound of tearing metal, the two wrecks were finally wrenched apart. From between them spilled a completely flattened Volkswagen Beetle—and the decomposing remains of the car's four passengers.

Trapped by Their Seat Belts

This story made the rounds in Wisconsin when the state legislature passed a mandatory seat belt law in 1987.

A stretch limo pulled up in front of a house in Dickeyville, Wisconsin, to carry five bridesmaids to church for a friend's wedding.

"Now promise me you'll all wear your seat belts," said the mother of one of the bridesmaids.

Her daughter rolled her eyes and sighed heavily, but the other young women all promised. The mother watched as the bridesmaids buckled themselves in, and then the limo driver pulled away from the curb and headed toward the church.

The driver paused at a stop sign and was halfway through the intersection when he heard the blare of a horn. He turned his head toward the direction of the sound, and saw an oil truck barreling down the street, headed straight for them. Before the driver could react, the out-of-control oil tanker smashed into the limo. The tanker ruptured from the impact and the oil burst into flames.

The limo driver was dead, but his five passengers were still alive and conscious. One of the bridesmaids threw open the car door and reached for the button of her seat belt. It would not release.

"I can't get out! I can't get out!" she screamed.

Nor could any of her friends.

They tugged frantically at their seat belts, and begged for help from the crowd of bystanders who rushed to the scene of the accident. But the burning oil kept any would-be rescuers at bay. The five trapped bridesmaids were still pleading for help and tugging furiously at their seat belts when the flames reached the limo's gas tank. The limo exploded in an enormous fireball, taking its "safely" belted-in passengers with it.

The Lost Car

A road construction crew was widening the highway to Miette Hot Springs in Alberta, Canada. One day, as they shoved rocks and boulders over the side of a deep ravine, they heard the clang of stone striking metal. Curious, the crew scrambled down the slope and began chopping through the underbrush.

Beneath the tangle of vines and bushes they found a car with license plates from 1950. Inside, still sitting upright and staring straight ahead, were the skeletons of the car's four passengers.

The wallets and handbags of the passengers were still intact. From these, police investigators established that these four people were a family that had vanished without a trace decades before. Their fate had been an unsolved mystery, until a road crew pushed some rocks off the edge of the ravine.

Variations: The original version of this legend dates to 16th-century Scandinavia. A hunter shoots an arrow at a pheasant and misses, but hears the clang of his arrow striking metal. With his hatchet, the hunter chops his way through the undergrowth. There, hidden beneath a thick canopy of centuries-old trees, he finds an abandoned stone church. Inside he discovers an entire congregation of skeletons scattered across the floor of the church, and the skeleton of a priest at the altar.

When the Black Death was sweeping across Scandinavia, the hunter's region of Norway had been especially hard hit. Whole villages had been wiped out. These villagers had gathered in their church with their priest, hoping they would be spared. But the plague found them, and here they remained unseen and forgotten, until by chance the hunter's arrow struck their church bell.

The DWI

One day after work, a man joined his friends for a drink at a bar in downtown San Diego. One drink became several, and although he was in no condition to be on the road, the drunk insisted he would drive himself home. His friends were not in much better shape, so they did not argue with him.

He wasn't on the road long before he was pulled over by a state trooper.

While the cop and the drunk were going through the standard license-and-registration procedure, a fender bender occurred a few hundred yards down the road.

"Just stay where you are," the cop instructed the drunk. "I've got to check out this accident. Then I'll be back and we'll finish up our business."

But after 15 minutes of waiting, the man got impatient. "The hell with it," he said, as he climbed into the car, drove home and locked the car in the garage.

Even in his sorry condition, the drunk knew he would be in serious trouble if the police found him.

"If the cops call," the man told his wife, "just tell them I was at home all night. I had a couple of drinks here and then went straight to bed. Promise you'll cover for me."

Reluctantly, the wife promised.

The next morning, two cops came to the door. One of them was the state trooper who had pulled the drunk over the night before.

"That's the guy who ran off last night," the trooper said to his fellow officer.

The man and his wife swore that the police had the wrong man.

"Folks, there's a simple way to settle this," said the other officer. "Would you mind opening your garage door?"

"What for?" the man asked.

"Sir, it will take just one quick look inside for us to determine if we've made a mistake."

So the husband and wife led the police to the garage. The wife punched in the security code and the door lifted. Inside the garage was a state trooper's car, its red and blue lights still flashing.

The Helpful Car-Stripper

A rash of car strippings in New York City inspired this legend.

One night before Christmas, as a man was driving home from a shopping mall, his car broke down on the Long Island Expressway on the outskirts of Queens. Cursing, he pulled over to the shoulder of the highway, climbed out of the car and popped open the hood. A moment later, another car pulled up behind him.

"Mind if I give you a hand?" the stranger asked.

"That'd be great," said the stranded motorist. "Thanks."

But rather than inspect the engine with the motorist, the good Samaritan walked to the back of the car. Like an expert, he jimmied open the trunk where he saw bags of merchandise from the motorist's holiday shopping spree.

So he yelled to the driver, "Here's the deal, buddy. You keep everything you can get out of the front, but the back of the car is mine."

The Microwave by the Side of the Road

This story originated in England when speed detectors were first introduced along the highways.

A woman was driving near Norwich when she spotted a large microwave oven abandoned by the side of the road. She suspected the microwave was probably not in working order, but she pulled over anyway. Her husband was an electrician and he might be able to repair it. The woman stowed the microwave in the back seat and headed home.

She was so proud of her find that she didn't notice she was exceeding the speed limit—until she heard the siren of a police car behind her.

Leaning in the window, the cop said, "You were traveling pretty fast, ma'am—" Then he saw the microwave in the back seat. "Where'd you get that, ma'am?"

"The microwave? I found it abandoned by the side of the road."

"Please step out of the car. You're under arrest for theft of government property."

As the officer led her toward the police car the woman protested. "Since when is a microwave government property?"

"That's no microwave, ma'am," the police officer replied. "That device checks motorists' speed. Into the back seat now. And mind your head."

Playing Chicken

A group of friends liked to take their motorcycles out at night and tear up and down back roads with their headlights off. One night they went to an access road that led to a quarry. One biker was having an especially good time. He had a new Harley that was outdistancing all of his friends' bikes.

At one point he shot away from the rest of the group and raced down the long dark road. At the quarry gates he stopped and turned his bike around. A long way back he could see two headlights.

"They've gone chicken," he thought. "They've switched on their lights."

He gunned his engine and tore back down the road, intending to dart between his two friends.

The headlights were blinding, but he increased his speed. He aimed dead center between the two headlights—and ran straight into the grille of a gravel truck.

Variation: An alternate version of this legend tells of a high school boy who likes to play chicken with oncoming cars. He sees a single headlight coming toward him, assumes it is a motorcycle and decides to give the biker a real scare. The kid goes barreling down the road—and straight into the grille of a truck with one blown headlight.

The Unrepentant Driver

At Christmastime, a man was circling a shopping mall parking lot looking for a place to park his Cadillac. He tried to squeeze into a space that was too small and wound up making a large dent in the fender of a Ford Escort.

The culprit's first impulse was to drive away. But the parking lot was filled with people, and a small crowd had stopped to observe what he would do next.

With a contrite expression on his face, he climbed out of his car, wrote something on a piece of paper and slipped it under the windshield. Then he got back into his Cadillac and drove away.

When the owner of the Escort got back to his car, he saw the dent first and then the scrap of paper on his windshield. He opened the note and read: "The people watching me think I'm leaving the name of my insurance company to cover the damage to your car. But I'm not."

Theft Takes a Holiday

During the week between Christmas and New Year's Day, a businessman was making the long drive from Seattle to Spokane. He was bored, so when he saw a hitchhiker along the side of the road, he pulled over and offered him a ride. As soon as the guy climbed into the car, the businessman regretted his decision. The hitchhiker was shabbily dressed, his hair was greasy and unwashed and he smelled bad.

When another hitchhiker appeared along the side of the road—a clean-cut, nicely dressed young man—the businessman pulled over again and offered the kid a ride. Now he relaxed. He figured the scruffy hitchhiker wouldn't try anything with two men in the car.

They hadn't traveled far before the kid pulled a pistol out of his backpack and ordered the driver to pull off the highway and drive down a dirt road.

"Give me the keys," he said. "Now get out of the car. Both of you."

He backed the driver and the scruffy hitchhiker away from the car. Waving the gun back and forth, he demanded their wallets and their watches. Suddenly, the scruffy hitchhiker lunged at the kid and knocked him cold with a single powerful blow to the head. He took the gun and went through the kid's pockets.

"Only forty bucks," the scruffy hitchhiker said. "From the way he was waving around that gun, I knew he was an amateur. But it's better than nothing. Here. You take a twenty," and he handed a $20 bill to the driver.

"What are you going to do now?" the driver said.

"Don't worry. I ain't gonna rob you," the scruffy hitchhiker said. "I don't work during the holidays."

The Sympathetic Car Thief

A man from Cape Town, South Africa, bought a new Porsche for his wife as a birthday present. As he was driving it home from the car dealer, it occurred to him that a big bouquet of flowers in the front seat might be a nice touch.

While the generous husband was in the florist's shop, a car thief spotted the spanking new Porsche. In a matter of minutes, he forced the lock, hot-wired the car and drove off. Soon afterwards, the husband stepped out of the shop with a large bunch of flowers and found the Porsche gone.

His first thought was to call the police, but then he recalled that he had had a car phone installed in the Porsche. He went back inside the florist shop, borrowed their phone and dialed the car phone's number. The thief picked up.

"Look," the husband said, "that car is a gift for my wife. It's her 30th birthday. While you were taking the Porsche, I was buying her flowers. Couldn't you be a sport and just leave the car in front of my house? My address is on the sales slip inside the glovebox. I promise I won't press charges."

"I'll give it some thought," the thief said. Then he hung up.

The florist asked if the husband wanted to call the police.

"No. I'll go home first and see what happens. You never know."

A little while later, a cab brought the husband home. There, sitting in front of his house, was the Porsche. With a big bouquet of flowers in the front seat.

The Bargain Corvette

This story made the rounds in the 1970s when "tiny" sports cars became popular on the American market.

In 1977 a woman whose son was killed in Vietnam called a used car dealer and offered to sell him the old car her son left behind.

"All I want is five hundred dollars for it," the woman said.

The dealer was sure that she was selling some jalopy, but he wanted to be kind to a grieving mother. "I'll tell you what," he said. "I'll come out to look the car over after lunch. Then let's see what kind of arrangement we can come to."

Early in the afternoon, the dealer arrived at the woman's house. She led him out to the garage and removed a tarp, revealing a gorgeous red 1967 Corvette sitting on wooden blocks, all the motor fluids drained from the engine.

"Ma'am, this is one beauty of a car. Why are you asking only five hundred? Don't you know you could get . . . a few hundred more for a car like this?"

"I don't see how anyone would pay more than five hundred dollars," the woman said. "The car's ten years old. And besides, it's so small."

The Adulterymobile

The owner of a small corporation in Munich was fined the equivalent of $300 for speeding on the Autobahn. She called the traffic police to dispute the penalty.

"The BMW cited in the summons is an office car," the executive said. "Any of a dozen of my employees could have been driving it. You have to prove that I was the one behind the wheel."

A few days later, a package arrived from the police. In it were radar trap photos. The pictures showed the executive at the wheel of the BMW—while a man nibbled her ear and fondled her naked breasts. The man was not her husband.

The police got their money. And the executive's husband got a divorce.

The Zombie in the Flatbed

On a dreary day outside Alexandra Township in South Africa, a driver for a coffin manufacturer stopped to give an old man a ride. The old fellow climbed into the flatbed of the truck. Suddenly the sky opened and sheets of rain came down. To get out of the wet, the old man climbed into a coffin.

While it was still raining, the driver saw another man, obviously very drunk, staggering along the side of the road. The driver stopped and offered him a lift. The drunk climbed into the flatbed and sat down among the coffins. When the rain stopped, the elderly man in the coffin raised the lid and began to climb out. Shrieking with terror, the drunk dove off the back of the truck.

The poor frightened man broke both his arms in the fall. When an ambulance crew found him, he insisted that he had jumped off a moving truck to escape a zombie.

"You're okay now," one of the paramedics said. "We'll get those broken bones patched up, and then you can rest up at the hospital."

Then, turning to another paramedic, he whispered, "Radio the psych ward that we've got a delivery for them."

"R" Is for Race

For his 17th birthday, a kid in Southern California received a new Camaro from his parents. That night, he picked up his girlfriend and they went out cruising.

At a stoplight in Malibu, they came alongside a Ford Mustang driven by a guy about the same age as the birthday boy. The drivers gunned their engines and exchanged a few insults. Then they decided to race.

The light turned green, and with a roar of dueling engines, the Mustang and the Camaro took off. After a few hundred yards, the Mustang pulled ahead.

"We're losing," the girlfriend complained.

"Don't worry. I've got a special gear."

"What are you talking about? There's no special gear—"

But before the girlfriend could finish, the kid shifted up. The transmission emitted a sickening grinding sound before the car spun out of control and slammed into a tree. Miraculously, neither the driver nor his girlfriend were hurt.

"You moron!" the girlfriend shrieked. "What did you do?"

"Nothing," her indignant boyfriend answered. "All I did was put it in 'race.'"

"Race! There's no gear for race, you idiot!"

"Oh yeah? Then what does the *R* stand for?"

The Phantom Speeder

A highway patrol officer near the Texas–Mexico border had a favorite speed trap on a dark country road. Late one night, his radar went off. It read "150," but the cop saw no car. He radioed another patrol car, but they saw no traffic on the road at all. So he dismissed the reading as a glitch.

The next day at the station, before he went on his shift, he checked his radar gun and found that it was working properly. After dark, he returned to his favorite spot. Sometime after two in the morning, the radar gun went off, this time reading "157." But again, the officer saw no car. He radioed another patrol car in the area. "You boys seen any speeding vehicles? I just clocked something at 157."

"We ain't seen nothing," said the other cop. "Are your phantom speeders out on the road again?"

A few minutes later, the cop with the "faulty" speed gun was called to the scene of an accident about ten miles down the road. Wrapped around a tree was a matte black Corvette. Its windows were tinted dark like a limousine and its lights were out.

Inside were two men, both dead. The driver was wearing night-vision goggles. In the trunk the police found three briefcases packed with cocaine.

"Boys," said the cop, "I think we just found my phantom speeders."

The Gas Thief

A college boy driving cross-country one summer ran out of gas on a dark stretch of road outside Bloomington, Indiana. It was after midnight. There were no gas stations in sight and no traffic on the road, so he pulled his empty gas can and a length of hose from his trunk and started walking. An hour later, he still hadn't found a gas station. Finally, he came upon a campground filled with RVs.

By now it was nearly two in the morning. Everyone in the campground was sound asleep. "I hate to do it," the kid said to himself, "but I'll have to siphon some gas from one of these RVs."

He crept up to the closest RV and tried to find the gas tank. By running his fingers over the bottom of the RV he found a cap. He twisted it off, slipped the hose into the tank and began to suck.

As soon as the liquid filled his mouth, the kid vomited violently.

Retching uncontrollably, still holding his gas can and the hose, he staggered out of the campground and into the night.

The next morning the father confronted his family in the RV. "Okay. Who left the cap off the septic tank last night?"

The Amateur on the Roof

A married couple in suburban New Jersey had a leaky roof. "Call a roofer," the wife said, "and ask him to come over and give you an estimate."

"Roofers cost a fortune," the husband said. "And they'll leave with the job half-finished. I can do it myself."

"I think you're out of your mind," said the wife. "But do what you want."

On Saturday morning, the husband climbed out the attic window and onto the roof. It was much higher than it looked from the ground, and the pitch of the roof was steeper than he had imagined. He climbed back in and wondered what he could rig to make himself feel more secure while he repaired the leak.

Then he had an idea.

From the basement he brought up a very long clothesline. He anchored one end of the rope to the attic window frame and tossed the other end over the peak of the roof. Then he went downstairs and out to the yard, where he tied the clothesline to the bumper of his car. Back at the attic window, he wrapped the other end of rope around his waist, tied it securely and climbed out on the roof to begin the repair job.

About 15 minutes later, his wife left the house. She never noticed the rope tied to the car's bumper. But as she drove away, she thought she heard something behind her go "splat."

The Fly and the Biker

A motorcyclist in rural Minnesota refused to wear a helmet. He loved the feel of the wind in his face and hair as he raced down the highway, and he wasn't going to give up that sensation.

His family and friends tried to talk sense into him. The highway patrol cops gave him one ticket after another. Even his fellow bikers urged him to wear a helmet. But he could not be persuaded.

"I've been riding for 15 years," he would say. "I've got great reflexes and I've never had an accident. So forget about helmets."

One hot summer day he was on his bike, speeding along his favorite stretch of road in the back woods of Minnesota. The road was empty. No cops were in sight. So he decided to take his Harley to the limit. At 150 miles per hour, something hit his eye. He lost control and flew off the bike into a ditch, where a passing motorist found him a few hours later. He was dead.

At the hospital the doctors sat down with the biker's distraught family. "It wasn't the crash that killed him. He was dead before he was thrown from the bike."

"Was it a heart attack, then?" the father asked.

"No. In fact, it was freak accident. A fly killed him. You see, your son was traveling at such high speed that when he hit a fly, it pierced right through his cornea and into his brain.

"The sad thing is," the doctor continued, "this tragedy could have been avoided if he had been wearing a helmet."

LATE FOR FINALS
AND OTHER TALES
FROM COLLEGE

Late for Finals and Other Tales from College

Late for Finals

Three students at Marquette University in Milwaukee blew off the entire weekend before final exams and indulged in heavy-duty partying. About noon on Monday, the boys woke up in their dorm room. They were all suffering from bad hangovers. Worse, they realized that their chemistry final had ended an hour ago.

"We're gonna fail! We're all gonna fail!" one of the three party boys said.

"Don't panic," said one of his friends. "All we need is a solid story to explain our absence."

A couple of hours later, they found their chemistry teacher in his office and explained that they had gone to Chicago for the weekend.

"On Sunday night, while we were driving home, we got a flat tire out in the middle of nowhere," one kid explained. "We didn't have a spare. The state police found us about an hour later, but by then it was two in the morning and no service station was open to replace the flat. So we had to spend the night in a motel. Then, the next morning, we had to have the car towed to a service station to get a new tire. We raced back to the school, but we didn't arrive in time for the final. Couldn't we please have an extension?"

"Yes, you can have an extension," the professor said. "Come here again tomorrow morning at ten. Of course, it will have to be a different exam than the one I gave the rest of the class today."

The next morning, the three happy students arrived at the professor's office for the exam. He handed each student a test booklet and sent them into separate rooms. The first question, worth 5 points, asked about molarity and solutions.

The second question, worth 95 points, read: "Which tire went flat?"

The Definition of Courage

A philosophy professor at Georgetown University was notorious for his brutal final examination questions. As the end of the semester approached, students in his ancient Greek philosophy class were studying furiously to prepare for the exam.

On the day of the final, the professor walked into the room and surveyed the room of nervous students. Without a word of introduction, he passed out the exam. There was only one question: "Define courage."

Every student in the examination room began to write furiously. Except one. He jotted something down, walked to the front of the room, handed his test to the professor and left.

The professor looked at the exam. Under the question "Define courage," the student had written, "This is."

The professor gave him an A.

Variations: The difficult final exam question is a staple among academic urban legends. In some legends, the question is long-winded and complex, generally beginning, "State succinctly whether or not you support the proposition that . . ." and ending with, "Support your answer with reasons." The student writes, "Yes. Because you do." The professor gives him an A. Another version, popular in divinity schools, tells of an elderly professor who for decades has asked the same question on his final exam: "List in chronological order the kings of Judah." Then one year he changes the question to: "List the major and minor prophets." One student tries to dodge the new question by writing, "Far be it from me to say which of those august personages was major and which was minor. Instead, permit me to name the kings of Judah."

"I Like It Better Each Time"

An English professor at Brown University was a notoriously tough grader. Few students in his class received anything higher than a D. But one bright kid labored for weeks on a ten-page paper about

Shakespeare's *Measure for Measure*. When the professor returned the term papers, the student was thrilled to see that he had received a B minus. He took the paper back to his room and hung it on the wall over his bed.

The next year the student joined a fraternity and he brought his prize paper with him. One Saturday night he held an auction and sold the paper to the highest bidder.

The frat brother who submitted it got a B. The next semester, another member of the frat bought the paper, turned it in and got a B plus. The semester after that, the scenario was repeated and this time the owner got an A.

Beneath the last grade the professor wrote this comment: "I've read this paper four times now, and I like it better each time. P.S.: I've notified the Dean—all four of you will be expelled."

"What Happened to the Pictures?"

An art major at a college in San Diego took a marine biology class. For his final project, he turned in a 20-page term paper on whales, complete with superb drawings of blue, sperm and humpback whales, with each part of the whales' anatomy clearly labeled and explained. The professor gave the student an A.

The next year the art student sold his paper to a friend who retyped it, but included the original drawings. He also received an A.

The year after that, a third student bought the paper and retyped it, but decided against including the drawings. He received a C, with a note from the professor: "What happened to the pictures?"

The Midnight Scream

For years, UCLA had a traditional "dead period," a solid week of silence on campus during finals week so students could study undisturbed. But in the 1960s a new tradition was born: the Midnight Scream. At the stroke of midnight on an appointed day, every student on campus would go outside or lean out their windows and scream for five minutes straight. It was supposed to be a great stress release.

At midnight on the day of the Scream, a young woman was racing down the back stairs of her dorm to join the shrieking crowd outside when she was grabbed from behind and dragged to the bottom of the stairwell. She screamed for help as she tried to fight off her attacker, but no one heard her in the commotion of the Midnight Scream. The next morning, her roommates found her battered corpse in the basement of their dorm.

Since then, UCLA has outlawed the Midnight Scream and many other colleges which once had the custom have followed suit.

A Matter of Taste

A college in Rochester, New York, offered a class known as "Bonehead Biology." It was a concession to students who had no other chance of passing the college's science requirement.

One day, the professor was lecturing on the human reproductive system. "One of the major components of male ejaculate, or sperm," he said, "is fructose. Fructose, you will recall, is a complex sugar."

A woman sitting in the front row of the lecture hall was perplexed, so she raised her hand.

"You have a question?" the professor said.

"I'm confused," the woman said. "If sperm is mostly sugar, then why does it taste so salty?"

Variation: In another version the biology instructor says that on average, a human male ejaculates only one teaspoon of sperm. The dimwitted student asks, "Then why does it make such a big mess?"

The Suicide Rule

The 1998 movie, Dead Man on Campus, *was inspired by this legend.*

As any college dorm resident can tell you, the easiest way to get a 4.0 for the semester is to have your roommate die. Murder, suicide, accidental death or a fatal illness all qualify, but the requirements vary from school to school.

Some schools insist that you must be present at the time of death. Surviving roommates who have not personally witnessed the death only get a 3.5 for the semester.

In other schools, the death must occur in the dorm room. In this case, the survivors can choose between a 4.0 for the semester, or first pick in the next dorm room lottery.

Some schools have rather stringent requirements. For example, the death must occur in the last six weeks of the semester.

Students who murder their roommates do not qualify for the automatic 4.0.

Variations: Students in some schools believe that the death of a parent or a sibling also qualifies for a 4.0. A related legend tells of a final exam in which a student killed himself. To console the other students in the room, the school gave them all an A for that exam.

Cakes and Ale

During a history final at England's ancient Cambridge University, the proctor saw a student raise his hand.

"Yes?" said the proctor.

"Sir, please bring me cakes and ale," the student said.

All the other students in the room stopped writing.

"Is this a joke?" the proctor asked.

"No sir. I request and require you to bring me cakes and ale."

"I will do no such thing. Continue with your examination."

"I am afraid, sir, that you must bring me cakes and ale," the student said. "The university's book of laws stipulates as much."

"I've never heard of such a thing," the proctor objected.

"Happily, I have a copy of the book with me," said the student. "You do read Latin, don't you?"

The student produced an ancient book and showed the relevant clause to the proctor. It read, "A student sitting for an examination may request and require the proctor to bring him cakes and ale."

"Very well," said the proctor. "I shall be back in a moment."

Twenty minutes later, the proctor returned with a serving tray. On it was a pitcher of ale, a glass and a small cake on a plate. "Here we are. May I borrow that book while you complete your exam?"

The student handed it over. The proctor returned to his desk at the front of the room and sat reading until the exam was over. Two hours later, the student brought his exam book up to the proctor.

"Thanks for the cakes and ale!"

"Just a moment," said the proctor. "I'm afraid you've violated one of the ancient laws of the university."

"What are you talking about?"

"Look here. It says very clearly, 'A student sitting for an examination who fails to wear his ceremonial sword shall be fined one pound.' You can pay the fine to me.' "

Variations: The setting for this story is always either Cambridge or Oxford. In other versions the student requests a glass of port or a jug of wine. Later, the proctor fines the student for failing to wear shoes with silver buckles, a tabard or a starched ruff collar.

The Letter Home

This urban legend has been circulating since the 1960s.

Dear Mom and Dad,

I can't believe it's been three months since I went off to college, and I can't believe it's taken me this long to write to you. But I have been VERY busy.

Now, before you read any further. I want you to sit down. Are you sitting? Okay. Here goes.

First of all, I am fine now. The doctors say the concussion I got when I dived out of the window during the dorm fire is healing nicely. Things were touch-and-go during those two weeks I spent in the hospital, but my eyesight is almost completely normal now, and I hardly ever get migraine headaches anymore.

Nobody died in the dorm fire, because Jimmy Ray, the night clerk at a 7-Eleven, saw the flames and called the fire department.

He called the ambulance for me, too. He came to see me every day in the hospital.

When I got out, Jimmy Ray invited me to live with him (since my dorm room was totally destroyed). It's a basement apartment, and he has it fixed up like a dungeon with chains and cages. And because almost everything I brought with me to school was burned up, Jimmy Ray bought me a lot of new clothes. He says I look great in black leather.

I've never met anyone like Jimmy Ray. He's so interesting, you'd never suspect he dropped out of school in the sixth grade. I have fallen in love with him and we have decided to get married. The wedding will be very soon, since the baby is due in seven months or so.

I was afraid we'd have to wait, because when we went for the blood test the lab found that Jimmy Ray had some kind of infection. But he says it's cleared up now.

I know you will welcome Jimmy Ray into the family. I just wish his family could be at the wedding, but his mother ran off with a door-to-door Bible salesman when Jimmy Ray was still a baby and it doesn't look like his daddy will make parole in time for the ceremony. Our society is so intolerant of repeat offenders.

Now that I have brought you up to date, I want to reassure you. There was no dorm fire. I did not suffer a concussion. I am not engaged. I am not pregnant. I don't even have a boyfriend. I am, however, getting a D in biology, an F in French, and I will have to repeat English Composition. I just wanted you to see that as bad as my first semester in college has been, it could have been a lot worse!

Your loving daughter,
Jenny

Variations: Other versions of this letter have a racist tone: the boyfriend is black or Latino. More recent editions of the letter include the suggestion that the daughter is involved in a lesbian relationship or has contracted AIDS.

The Obligatory Waiting Period

Virtually all college students believe that their school has a policy known as the "obligatory waiting period," which specifies how long students must remain in the classroom before leaving if the instructor fails to appear. In some schools the waiting time is based on the academic rank of the instructor.

Teaching Assistants: 5 minutes.

Visiting lecturers and non-tenured faculty: 10 minutes.

Tenured faculty: 15 minutes.

If His Hat Is There, Then He's There

A math professor at MIT got to class early. As he placed his hat on his desk, he remembered that he had left some papers in his office.

But on the way back to the classroom, the chairman of the department stopped him and talked to him at length about new office assignments for tenured faculty. By the time the professor returned, it was fifteen minutes into the class period and the students were gone.

The next day, as the bell rang to announce the beginning of class, the professor strode to the podium. "You had no excuse for leaving class," he said.

"But professor," one of the students said, "you were not there. We waited the full 15 minutes."

"Nonsense. Didn't you see my hat on the desk? If my hat was there, it meant I was there." Then he proceeded with the day's lecture.

The next day when the professor arrived at class, he found the room empty. But on each desk was a hat.

He Should Have Been More Specific

The professor of an introductory English literature course at Duke University announced that the upcoming final examination would be an open-book test. "You can use whatever you can carry into the classroom," he said.

A week later, on the day of the exam, one student entered the classroom carrying a doctoral candidate in English literature.

The Off-Color Professor

This story dates from the early 1970s when the rise of the feminist movement on college campuses inspired many urban legends.

An anatomy professor at the University of Wisconsin often enlivened his lectures with suggestive anecdotes. A group of women from his class came to his office one day to complain.

"We've had enough of your snide, leering, adolescent humor," the spokesperson said. "The next time you say anything even remotely off-color, we will walk out of the room."

The professor listened in silence. Then he said, "As you wish, ladies."

For several weeks the professor was the model of decorum. Then one day he began his lecture saying, "As you know, France is suffering from a sudden shortage of prostitutes."

Before he could say another word, a dozen women in the room rose and headed for the door.

"Ladies," said the professor, "why the rush? The next plane for Paris doesn't leave until ten this evening."

The Surprise Visitors

Two college kids who were notorious for playing practical jokes on each other roomed together at Villanova. One Saturday afternoon, one of the guys came back to the room after his run. He stripped off his sweaty clothes, grabbed a towel and headed down the hall to the shower.

A few minutes later, there was a knock at the door. It was the runner's girlfriend with her parents. They had dropped by for a surprise visit to see their daughter and meet her boyfriend. The roommate closed the door and asked them to take a seat. "He just stepped out. He'll be back soon."

Meanwhile, the runner came padding down the hall from the shower. Outside his room, he dropped his towel and kicked open the door. With his penis in his right hand, he burst into the room shouting, "My enormous heat-seeking moisture missile lays waste to everything in its path!"

Football Is for the Birds

A student at the University of Nebraska did not make the cut for the football team. When he asked why, the coach was brutally honest. "You're too short, you're slow and you can't catch the ball."

Angry and humiliated, the student went back to his dorm and plotted his revenge.

He got a campus job for the summer, then called his parents and told them he would be spending the vacation on campus.

The next day, he put on a black-and-white striped shirt, took a large bag of birdseed and headed over to the football field. He blew a whistle, then stepped onto the field and scattered birdseed for the next half hour. Every day, rain or shine, all summer long, he would put on his black-and-white striped shirt, blow his whistle and scatter birdseed across the football field.

When Nebraska played its first home game the student was sitting in the stands. As the national anthem ended, the referee stepped onto the field and blew his whistle. Immediately, hundreds of birds flew out of the sky and landed on the field, waiting for their daily ration of birdseed.

Short Takes

• A wealthy ice cream manufacturer made a generous bequest to Harvard with one string attached: Ice cream had to be served at every lunch and dinner.

• The parents of a Swarthmore College student who drowned donated a swimming pool to the school with the stipulation that all students be required to pass a swimming test to graduate.

• The mother of a Harvard student who drowned on the *Titanic* donated a new library building to the school with the stipulation that all students be required to pass a swimming test to graduate.

• Carnegie-Mellon University has the second highest workload and the second highest suicide rate of all American universities.

• As a prank, the registrar at Yale filled an entire class with students whose last names were also the names of animals, such as Byrd, Fox, Lyon, Finch and Lamb.

• A Harvard professor gave a final exam with only one question on it: "Why?" Students who answered "Why not?" got an A. "Because" got a B. Everyone else flunked.

• Henry Kissinger, Class of 1950, was the last Harvard student to graduate with straight A's.

• The University of Utah library is sinking because the architect who designed the building failed to allow for the weight of the books.

• When *Playboy* magazine ranked the top ten party schools, the University of Wisconsin did not appear on the list. The editors explained, "We don't rank professionals with amateurs."

• A shrewd student financed his college education by asking everyone he met for a penny. He got enough to cover all his expenses and go away for Spring Break every year. When he graduated, he had $28,000 in the bank.

Aliens in Roswell, New Mexico and Other Close Encounters

ALIENS IN ROSWELL, NEW MEXICO AND OTHER CLOSE ENCOUNTERS

Aliens in Roswell

In July 1947 residents of Roswell, New Mexico, saw something odd streak across the sky and crash outside town. The first witnesses to arrive on the scene were two sheep ranchers who swore that they found the wreckage of some type of strange aircraft. The ranchers said fragments of the aircraft bore symbols or letters unlike anything they had ever seen.

Meanwhile, the mortuary officer at the Army base nearby called a Roswell funeral home and asked the director if he could procure some small airtight caskets. Then the Army officer asked for advice on how to preserve bodies without contaminating the tissue. The funeral director drove out to the base to see if he could help. When he arrived he saw large pieces of metal inscribed with odd markings sticking out from the back of a military ambulance. Then he went inside to say hello to a nurse he knew on the base. When the guards spotted the funeral director, they forced him to leave.

The next day the nurse came to the funeral director's office. "You know those little caskets you brought over yesterday?" she said. "They're for spacemen."

"What are you talking about?" the funeral director asked.

"A flying saucer crashed outside town and the Army retrieved these bodies. I saw them," the nurse said. "This is what they look like." She pulled a prescription pad from her pocket and drew pictures of small, thin men with elongated heads.

Not long afterwards the nurse was transferred to a base in England. She has never been heard from since.

After sending out an intelligence officer to examine the crash site, the base commander issued a press release on July 8, 1947, stating that the wreckage of a crashed flying saucer had been recovered near Roswell. The following day, an Army spokesman retracted the story and said that the wreckage had in fact been a weather balloon.

But the residents of Roswell who were at the site still maintain that they can tell the difference between five pounds of balsa wood and conventional aluminum foil, and the otherworldly debris that was strewn across their fields.

Aliens Among Us

Only a few months after the recovery of alien bodies and the debris from their spacecraft at Roswell in 1947, President Harry S. Truman created MJ-12, a top-secret organization to collect intelligence on UFOs.

In 1954 President Dwight D. Eisenhower expanded the mandate of MJ-12 by founding the clandestine Jason Society, a hand-picked group of scholars charged with evaluating data about UFOs and contact with alien life forms. Members of the secret society have included Allen Dulles, director of the CIA; Dr. Zbigniew Brzezinski, president of the Trilateral Commission from 1973 to 1976; and Dr. Henry Kissinger, the mastermind of America's foreign policy.

MJ-12 is funded by profits from the drug trade (MJ-12 members insist the drug trade is simply a tool to eliminate the weaker members of society). The power of MJ-12 has grown to the extent that it manipulates the CIA and the FBI; early in its history it monitored individuals through the mail and the telephone, and today it uses the latest computer technology to accomplish the same task.

Through a project code-named SIGMA, MJ-12 first made contact with aliens. MJ-12's PLATO project established diplomatic relations with several alien civilizations and even secured formal treaties with them. Special operatives known as Men in Black are responsible for the security of all aliens and alien spacecraft currently on earth.

The Real Men in Black

The Men in Black (commonly known as MIBs) have one job: To intimidate anyone who has seen a UFO and prevent them from talking about their experience.

As their name suggests, MIBs always wear a black suit, a thin black tie and an immaculate white dress shirt. Their voices are monotone. Their faces betray no emotion. They usually travel in vintage black Cadillacs, in mint condition. This was how the MIBs looked when they appeared at the door of a man in Toledo, Ohio, named Shepherd.

Three days earlier, Mr. Shepherd had been driving home when he came around a bend and saw a large, strange metallic object blocking the road. He hit the brakes, but could not stop in time and collided with the object. But at the moment of impact, it disappeared.

Shepherd called the police who inspected the scene with him. The front of Shepherd's car was damaged from the collision, and there were skid marks from his tires on the road. But there was no sign of the other vehicle. The police filed an accident report and Shepherd filed a claim with his insurance company. It seemed that the strange incident would be forgotten.

But Shepherd could not forget what happened. He returned to the scene of the accident, and this time he found a piece of metal unlike any kind of metal he had ever seen before. He sent it to a metallurgical lab for analysis.

Three days later, at 11 PM, two MIBs appeared at Shepherd's door. Over their shoulders, Shepherd could see their car—a black

1953 Cadillac. They asked Shepherd a few questions, and then they asked him for the piece of metal he'd found at the accident site.

"I don't have it anymore," Shepherd said. "I've sent it to a lab for analysis."

"If you want your wife to stay healthy," one of the MIBs said, "then you better not mention that fragment to anyone."

Shepherd was stunned—by the threat and by the MIBs knowledge of his find. Only his wife and the lab knew about the fragment. Still, he took the threat seriously. The first thing the next morning, Shepherd called the lab and asked them to return the fragment. The technician he spoke to said they had no such fragment, never had such a fragment and that no one in the lab had ever had any contact with Mr. Shepherd.

Variations: Some legends tell of a doctor who was acting as a consultant in an alien abduction case was visited by MIBs. To demonstrate their power and convince him to withdraw from the investigation, they made a coin dematerialize. Others claim that a Canadian man who saw a UFO was visited by MIBs who warned him not to talk about his experience if he valued the life of his wife and children.

Abducted by Aliens

One morning, a woman from Alabama awoke from a terrifying dream. Over breakfast, she described it to her mother and brother. She had seen herself in a circular room in some type of spaceship. She was lying on a table, naked and powerless. Standing around her were small white creatures with large black eyes who were performing medical procedures on her that she did not understand.

The woman's family dismissed it as a nightmare, but after the dream became more frequent and more intense, they suggested that she see a psychiatrist who specialized in hypnotic regression. Under hypnosis, the woman recalled that she had been abducted by aliens several times. And the abductions have continued.

She has found strange marks on her body, including signs that she had been stuck with sharp instruments. She often hears odd beeping sounds, similar to Morse code. Furthermore, after she has an "abduction dream," she suffers from soreness in her ovaries that lasts for several weeks.

The woman believes that she is being monitored by her abductors. Her telephone emits strange sounds that phone company repairmen cannot explain nor correct. Her home security system shuts down spontaneously—again, repair crews have never been able to locate the source of the problem. Sometimes, the woman's house reverberates with unearthly sounds.

The psychiatrist was disturbed by what his patient revealed under hypnosis, so he ran a battery of psychological tests to determine if she had any delusional tendencies. The test results showed that the woman was normal; in fact, they indicated that she was less likely than most people to indulge in daydreams or fantasies.

Variations: Many alien abduction stories begin with the subject recalling how he or she passed easily and painlessly through solid matter such as the roof of their home or car, and floated up to an awaiting spacecraft. The aliens that abduct the humans are described as short creatures of whitish, grayish or bluish hue. Once the human is aboard the spacecraft, an alien the abductees generally refer to as "the doctor" takes over. Assisted by others, the doctor performs intricate procedures on the abductee. The medical procedures include forcing the abductee to swallow a strange liquid; drawing the brain from the skull and examining it; implanting small objects within various parts of the body; and drawing samples of blood, tissue, marrow and bodily fluids. Many male abductees say a device was placed over their testicles and penis for the collection of semen, while female abductees describe a similar device that collected their ova.

Aliens Collect Blood Samples

Two men who worked at a casino in Buenos Aires, Argentina, were driving home at the end of their shift when they saw two metallic disks that resembled upside-down soup bowls hovering over an empty lot.

At the same time, the car's electrical system failed. Then the engine died. The next thing the two men knew, a beam of unearthly light emerged from the disks and struck the car. A door panel opened in one of the disks, and three small bald-headed creatures came gliding on the beam of light toward the car.

The creatures communicated with the two men telepathically. The two men understood the creatures to say that they had come to study Earth civilization and to collect blood samples of its various life forms. Then the men lost consciousness. When they came to, they saw a dazzling flash of light as the disks soared into the sky.

The men were about to dismiss the entire experience as a hallucination when they noticed pain in their index fingers. They each looked and saw traces of blood around a large puncture wound.

Mutilated Cattle

In 1973 a Kansas cattle rancher discovered a dozen of his cows dead and grotesquely mutilated. All the blood had been drained from their bodies. Their hearts, lungs, kidneys and reproductive organs had been surgically removed. Perhaps strangest of all, scavengers such as coyotes and buzzards had not touched the corpses.

The rancher called the local police, who notified the FBI. An investigation of the site found unusually high radiation levels around the dead cattle. The evidence of clamp marks on the animals' rear legs suggested that the cattle had been taken someplace where they had been suspended by their hind legs and mutilated before their bodies were dumped back in the pasture.

Some ranchers thought a crazy hippie cult or devil worshippers were to blame. But as the wave of cattle mutilations spread across the West, other evidence began to emerge. Witnesses saw UFOs or strange unmarked black helicopters hovering over herds.

Since that first incident, 10,000 head of cattle have been mutilated. To this day, no one knows who has been carving up the cows or their motivations.

Variation: One theory holds that "mad cow disease" was brought to Earth by aliens. After vivisecting cattle, they learned how best to infect the cows and, in turn, humans.

Crop Circles

In the 1970s outside the town of Warminster in England, a farmer awoke one morning to find that portions of his wheat crop had been flattened into perfect circles of various sizes. When he examined the damage, the farmer found that the stalks of wheat were only bent, not broken. In fact, the wheat continued to grow in the swirling circular pattern until harvest.

Soon crop circles began to appear in fields in Canada, the United States, Hungary, Russia, Australia and Japan. As the phenomenon spread around the globe, the patterns in the fields became more geometrically complex: rings, lines, squares and triangles also appeared.

In 1991 two men admitted to creating some 250 crop circles. But the circles these two hoaxers made had always been suspect— they lacked the precision and intricacy that were the hallmarks of this phenomenon.

Although no one knows exactly how these crop circles were created, several farmers observed bright disks of light hovering over their crops in the night. When the farmers inspected their fields, they found crop circles in the precise spot where the light had been the night before.

Variations: Whoever—or whatever—makes crop circles seems to prefer fields of corn, although the circles have also been found in fields of barley and oats. Sometimes the stalks are woven together. In other versions, the bottom stalks swirl in one direction while the stalks on top swirl in another direction. There have also been reports of multiple layers swirling in different directions. Electronic equipment is said to malfunction inside crop circles and magnets lose their magnetism.

Bar Codes and the Mark of the Beast

Top-level government researchers have been laboring for years to create a microchip which would be encoded with an individual's complete personal and medical history. To display this information, all one would have to do is pass a scanner over the chip.

But this research also has a sinister side. A lethal virus would be programmed into the chip. Since the implant would emit a signal that could be monitored through a cellular system or even by satellite, governments could eliminate criminals, the chronically ill, the disabled, dissidents or other "undesirables" by causing the chip to melt within the person's body, thus releasing the deadly virus.

Once the chip was developed, everyone on the planet would be required to have it implanted under their skin. Anyone who refused the implant would be exiled from society, denied employment and all civil rights and liberties.

Some biblical scholars have interpreted the development of the implant as the fulfillment of the apocalyptic prophecy of "the mark of the Beast"—the mark of those who reject God in the last days of the world and are subsequently damned for eternity.

The Battle of Los Angeles

On a moonless night in February 1942, just eight weeks after the attack on Pearl Harbor, a young Los Angeles woman who had volunteered as an air raid warden looked out her living room window and saw a massive aircraft that gave off a golden-orange light hovering above the city. Los Angeles was observing blackout regulations every night, so the craft appeared in the sky with wonderful clarity.

"I imagined it was some type of superweapon belonging to the Japanese," the woman recalled later. "And I should have been afraid of it. But it was so beautiful suspended in the night sky."

The next thing the air raid warden saw were Army fighter planes attacking the object. They flew in beautiful formation, fired at the craft and then swerved away. Wave after wave of fighters fired everything they had, but they made no impact on the object. As the planes fell back, the artillery batteries on the ground opened fire.

For half an hour, the guns blasted the object with high-explosive shells. Hundreds of eyewitnesses—by now the entire city was watching the battle—claimed they saw at least a dozen direct hits, but the craft showed no signs of damage. Nor did it return fire.

Suddenly, the golden orange light began to pulse in slow, rhythmic waves. Then the mysterious aircraft disappeared.

Fighting a UFO in Korea

One night during the Korean War in 1951, as an American infantry battalion bombarded an abandoned village, the soldiers saw a strange object that emitted an orange light descend the mountain and head into the village. It seemed impervious to artillery fire. For the next hour, the men watched in amazement as the glowing thing glided unscathed amid the inferno.

Then the object moved out of the village and approached the American batteries in the hills. Suddenly the light changed from orange to blue-green. And instead of a steady glow, it began to pulse. One of the men received permission from his commander to fire on the object. He took an M-1 rifle and fired off several rounds of armor-piercing bullets. The sharpshooter was surprised to hear the sound of a bullet piercing metal. The object may have been untroubled by artillery, but rifle fire was apparently another story.

Suddenly, the object went wild. It moved erratically from side to side and its lights flickered. Then it attacked.

Powerful rays of brilliant light shot out of the object, sweeping across the troops like a searchlight. Officers ordered the men to fall back to their bunkers. For the next half hour, the object hovered over the bunkers, discharging wave upon wave of dazzling light. Then it vanished.

When the attack was over, the men felt burning, tingling sensations throughout their bodies. By dawn, they were all suffering from dysentery and were so weak that the entire company had to be evacuated by ambulance. At the field hospital, doctors found that all of the men had unusually high white blood cell counts. Within three days, every member of the company was dead.

Alien Antiwar Activists

In March 1967, the commander of an Inter-Continental Ballistic Missiles (ICBM) site in Montana received a call from a security guard, who said that he and several other guards had seen UFOs above the military installation. The commander was skeptical, but told the guards to call him again if the situation changed. Five minutes later, the commander's phone rang again. It was the same guard.

"Sir! There's a disk-shaped aircraft emitting a red glow hovering above our front gate."

A moment later, the commander's second phone rang. An officer in the missile launch bunker reported, "Sir! The missiles are shutting themselves down. They've gone from Alert to No-Go status. We can't determine the cause of the failure."

Twenty miles away, the commander of another missile site found that his ICBMs were also shutting themselves down. Since there was no command in the launch bunker that could turn off the weapon systems, the commander was mystified.

For three hours the missiles were out of commission. Then, just as suddenly as they had shut down, the ICBMs came back on line. No repair work had been done on the system. An investigation found no broken cables or damaged hardware. Even the contractors from Boeing and Sylvania who had built the system could not determine what happened to the missiles. In fact, when the Boeing and Sylvania teams tried to duplicate the shutdown, they failed.

UFO watchers have offered possible reasons for the mysterious event. Some say the extraterrestrials who visited the missile sites may have come to urge humankind to abandon its weapons of mass destruction. Others insist that the aliens wanted to demonstrate how feeble our technology is compared to their own—perhaps as a warning that an alien invasion is imminent.

The Australian Fireball

In October 1994, a family in Western Australia had gathered on their patio for a barbecue when they saw a large ball of fire hurtling directly overhead.

"Everyone into the house!" the mother cried. "Now!"

Meanwhile the father called the local police station. "Jack! Look outside. A jet airliner is on fire and about to crash!"

The two cops ran out to the street just in time to see the fireball pass over the police station. By now the entire town of 4,000 people was outdoors watching the phenomenon.

Observing it straight on, the police thought the front appeared to be a dense mass of reddish orange flames. Residents who saw the fireball from the side said it trailed yellowish white flames. The family of barbecuers, now back on their patio and looking at the fireball as it passed right above them, described flames swirling inward and disappearing into a kind of vortex or black hole. From their perspective, this was more a ring of fire than a fireball.

For seven minutes or so, the inhabitants of this small town watched the fireball rocket across the sky. Then with a flash of bright blue flame, it accelerated. In an instant, the fireball was gone.

The Hiker and the Humanoids

This report appeared in the early 1970s.

An Australian hiker was camping near Warragamba Dam in New South Wales, about 110 miles from Sydney. One night, just as he was getting ready to turn in, he heard a loud humming sound. He took his flashlight and walked into the bush to find the source of the noise.

He had only walked a few hundred feet when he saw a brilliant white light up ahead. He turned off the flashlight and edged forward on his hands and knees. Between the trees he saw a large clearing. In the center was a strange egg-shaped structure that was giving off the bright light. Scurrying around it were half a dozen humanoid creatures.

After an hour or so, the creatures entered the egg. Suddenly the humming sound ceased and the egg vanished.

UFO Escorts

A United Airlines DC-3 was flying from Salt Lake City to Seattle when the copilot flashed the landing lights. When the captain asked him what he was doing, the copilot answered, "Don't you see it? There's an aircraft off our bow."

The captain looked and saw a strange disk-shaped craft. Suddenly, four more flying disks came into view. He called the flight attendant on the intercom. "Look out of the cabin windows. Tell me what you see out there."

The flight attendant came back on the intercom. "What are those things? And don't tell me we're being followed by flying saucers."

The captain radioed the nearest station on the ground and asked if they were picking anything up on radar. The reply came back, "Negative. The skies around you are clear."

The captain, his copilot and the stewardess observed the five disks for another 15 minutes. Then the disks disappeared.

The Great Martian Face

In the 1970s, when *Viking* spacecraft sent photographs of Mars back to Earth, one picture showed a formation that resembled a human face in an area now known as Cydonia. The two eyes, the broad nose and the mouth of the face can be seen clearly. In addition, all around the face are mounds that bear a striking resemblance to pyramids found in Egypt and Mesoamerica.

The initial reaction to the Cydonia Face was that it was a kind of extraterrestrial Rorschach test, the martian equivalent of the Man in the Moon. But in the decades since the first Viking photos of the face arrived on Earth, some scientists have re-evaluated their initial conclusions.

• The face does not resemble a face because of the play of light and shadow. There are actual three-dimensional contours to the structure.

• Military software designed to detect man-made objects—even if they are camouflaged—register the face as a structure built by living beings.

• Mounds are rare on the martian surface, but they are numerous in the Cydonia region. There is also a regular pattern to them that cannot simply be dismissed as chance.

• Finally, the face appears at a significant location on Mars—its equator.

The Cydonia face is too far away to be seen by viewers on Earth. In fact, the face cannot be detected even with the most powerful telescopes. This has led researchers to believe that the face was meant to be seen from some other point in the solar system—presumably the home planet of the face's builders.

Ancient Peru: First in Flight

In the late 1960s and early 1970s a researcher named Erich von Daniken argued that either the Inca or the pre-Inca civilization of ancient Peru had the technology to build and pilot aircraft. Von Daniken came to this conclusion during an archaeological dig when he found a miniature "airplane" in an ancient Peruvian grave.

Skeptics dismissed von Daniken's discovery and insisted that the figurine was really some type of mythical insect. But two German engineers decided to test von Daniken's theory. They built an aircraft with a propeller according to the model found in the Peruvian tomb. Then, with witnesses and a video camera on hand to record the event, the two engineers launched their airplane.

It flew!

Ancient Egyptian Flying Machines

What technology did the ancient Egyptians use to build the pyramids at Giza? How could they have lifted those immense blocks

214 • Alligators in the Sewer

of stone? Such questions have perplexed historians and archaeologists for centuries.

In the early 1970s some theorists advanced the idea that extraterrestrial visitors assisted the Egyptians in their massive building projects.

The notion has been dismissed by almost everyone in the academic community. But in the early 1990s, an Egyptologist made an astonishing find in the ancient Egyptian city of Abydos. In an ancient temple, she found carvings of strange flying machines—including one that bears a strong resemblance to a helicopter—a craft which would have been ideal in lifting the blocks of stone that built the pyramids.

THE BARREL OF BRICKS AND OTHER ON THE JOB FOIBLES

The Barrel of Bricks and Other On the Job Foibles

The Barrel of Bricks

This classic legend has been made into the Irish ballad "Why Paddy Won't Be in to Work Today."

A bricklayer was working alone on the roof of a new six-story building. When the job was done, he had quite a few bricks left over. Rather than carry the bricks down by hand, he decided to put them all in an empty barrel he had with him on the roof and lower the barrel using a pulley the construction crew had attached to the side of the building.

The bricklayer tied a heavy rope around the barrel and dropped the loose end of the rope over the side of the building. Then he went down and secured that end of the rope at ground level. Back up on the roof, the man swung the barrel out and began to load the bricks. When the barrel was full, the bricklayer descended again and untied the rope from its moorings intending to lower the barrel of bricks slowly to the ground. But the bricklayer had made one miscalculation. The barrel full of bricks weighed a little over 300 pounds, while the bricklayer tipped the scales at 195.

When he untied the rope, he was jerked swiftly into the air.

In his surprise and fright, he didn't think to let go of the rope. At the third floor the bricklayer and the barrel of bricks collided, breaking the man's collarbone and fracturing his skull.

As the barrel of bricks plummeted, the bricklayer kept ascending and did not stop until he had driven the fingers of his right hand two knuckles deep into the pulley.

At the same moment, the barrel of bricks hit the pavement with such impact that the bottom fell out. Now it was the bricklayer who outweighed the empty barrel. As he began to drop, the barrel flew upward. Once again they collided at the third floor. This time the bricklayer came away with a broken ankle.

When he hit the pile of bricks on the ground, the bricklayer finally let go of the rope. And he looked up just in time to see the empty barrel hurtling back down at him.

"Are You Gay?"

A USAir employee named David Gay took advantage of his company's "Employees Fly Free" program for a flight to Hawaii. When Mr. Gay made his way to his seat, he found it occupied by a paying passenger. Rather than make a fuss, he took an empty seat further back in the plane.

Meanwhile, another USAir plane, also flying to Hawaii, was experiencing mechanical difficulties. The passengers from this flight were being redirected to other airlines and a few were coming aboard Mr. Gay's plane. As a result, the flight attendants were instructed to review their passenger list and "bump" anyone who was holding a free ticket.

Armed with her passenger list, a flight attendant approached the seat assigned to Mr. Gay and asked the man, "Are you Gay?"

The man was silent for a moment. Then he said, "Yes. What of it?"

"I'm sorry. You'll have to get off the plane."

A few rows back, Mr. Gay overheard this conversation. He stood up and said, "You've got the wrong man. I'm Gay."

Then a third man stood up and yelled, "Hell, I'm gay, too. They can't kick us all off!"

The Gullible Tourist

Lake Louise, near Banff, Alberta, is a remarkably deep shade of blue. The color is so striking that it almost seems artificial.

On the shore of the lake is a five-star hotel, the Chateau Lake Louise. One day an American guest at the hotel came down to the beach and approached the lifeguard. "I've never seen anything so beautiful," she said. "What makes the lake so blue?"

The lifeguard thought he would have a little fun with the lady, so he said, "It's the paint they use. Every year, on September 22, we drain the lake and paint the bottom a vivid shade of blue. It takes weeks of hard work, but I think it's worth the effort, don't you?"

The American woman was astonished and didn't question the lifeguard's story. That night, the lifeguard had a laugh about his tall tale with his friends. The American woman left a couple days later and the lifeguard forgot all about the incident.

Two months later, on September 21, the same American woman approached the lifeguard on the beach. "Well, as you can see, I've come back," she said.

"Ma'am?"

"For the painting of the lake bottom, of course. And I've brought lots of film to record the event."

The Greedy Dealer

A dealer at a blackjack table in Atlantic City was bored with his job and unhappy about his pay. The owner of the casino believed that at least a third of a dealer's income should come from tips from the players and he paid his employees accordingly.

The blackjack dealer hated pandering to the players who came to his table, but he didn't know what else he could do to supplement his income. Then one afternoon, when things were a little slow, he took a silver dollar from the stack in front of him and dropped it down his pants leg and into his cowboy boot.

It worked beautifully. Nobody noticed. The dealer knew he was on to something. At the end of his shift, he walked out of the casino with $20 in his boots.

It was easy. In fact, it was too easy, and the dealer got greedy. He spent an entire shift slipping coins into his boots. When it was time to leave, he was carrying $200 in silver.

But the dealer hadn't counted on the weight of all those coins. He'd barely gotten three steps away from his table when he tripped— and all the silver dollars spilled out of his boots, scattering across the casino floor.

Unbleached Salmon

An entrepreneur in Alaska wanted to start up a canned salmon business. Since he was low on cash, he looked for ways to cut his expenses. A commercial fisherman told him that white salmon was considerably cheaper than pink salmon.

The entrepreneur bought several tons of white salmon and went into business. He was very happy, but his marketing manager was not.

"We took the white salmon to focus groups," he told the entrepreneur. "Consumers are turned off by the stuff. They're too used to pink salmon. What are we going to do?"

"Give me a day or two to think about this," the entrepreneur said.

Two days later, the entrepreneur came back to his marketing manager. "I have the solution. Start an ad campaign that says, 'Guaranteed not to turn pink in the can.'"

"That won't work," the marketing manager said.

"Humor me. Try it and see."

In fact, the campaign was an enormous success. The white salmon business took off, while canneries that sold pink salmon saw their sales plummet.

For several months, the white salmon entrepreneur was a very happy man. Then one day he was in a supermarket and he saw his competitor's canned pink salmon. A large banner across the label read: "Guaranteed: No bleach used in processing"!

The Last Kiss

This is one of the rare urban legends that originated in New Zealand.
A newly married man named Nelson had a job at a quarry as part of a team that worked the rock crusher. One day, a couple of weeks after his wedding, he slipped as he was stepping over the conveyor belt and was dragged into the machine. His friends managed to turn the machine off, but it didn't look good for Nelson.

The medic assessed the situation, gave Nelson some painkillers and then took the foreman aside.

"Here's what we've got. He's been chewed up from the waist

down. Even if we get him to the hospital alive, he'll be dead in a couple of hours. But if we turn the machine back on, it will all be over in a couple of seconds. What do you want to do?"

"I can't make that kind of decision," the foreman said. "I'll have to ask Nelson."

Nelson chose the quick way out. "But get my wife down here first. I want one last kiss before I go."

The foreman himself brought Nelson's wife to the quarry. The team went behind the stone crusher so the couple could have a few final minutes of privacy. At last, they saw Nelson's wife run from the quarry, sobbing.

"We're clear," the foreman said. Then, with his voice choked with emotion, he gave the order, "Start her up!"

Variation: The American version of this story is identical in all the details except one: In the U.S. telling, the man is trapped beneath a steamroller.

The Missing Fingers

This legend may go back to the 19th century and the heyday of the lumbering industry in Maine.

A man operated a large saw in a lumber mill in Maine. One day his attention wandered and he accidentally severed two fingers on his left hand. When he recovered he came back to the mill and resumed his old job on the same large saw. He worked for many years without ever having another accident.

One day, a group of high school students from Bangor came to the lumber mill for a tour. Eventually, they came to the large saw. One young woman noticed that the man was missing two fingers on his left hand.

"You poor man," she said. "Did you lose your fingers in an accident on the job?"

"That's right, miss. About thirty years ago, I lost my fingers on this very machine."

"That's terrible," she said. "How did it happen?"

"Like this," he replied. And he promptly cut off two more fingers.

Variation: The Texas version of this story tells of a farmhand who was careless with a posthole digger and sliced off two of his toes. When the farmer asked the poor guy how he could have done such a thing, the farmhand showed him and promptly lopped off another toe.

The Frustrated Bookkeeper

This story dates to 19th-century England. W. Somerset Maugham used it as the basis of his short story "The Verger."

A 17-year-old boy from the country traveled to London to seek his fortune, but he had no luck finding honest work. He was desperate when he wandered into London's red light district. Seeing no alternative, he walked up to a bordello, knocked on the door and asked for a job.

"I have work for you," the madam said. "I need a bookkeeper."

The boy was heartbroken. "I can't take the job," he said. "I can't read or write."

"That's a shame. But take these at least. You look hungry." And the madam handed the boy half a dozen apples.

Back on the street, the boy noticed that one of his shoelaces had come untied. He put the apples down on a wooden crate and knelt to tie his shoe. Suddenly he heard a man's voice say, "How much for the apples, boy?"

The boy was startled, but he thought fast. "Two pennies apiece, sir."

The man bought all six apples. With his 12 pennies, the boy ran to a fruit wholesaler at Covent Garden where he bought more apples. Soon, he parlayed his street-corner fruit stand into a grocery store, and from there he became the owner of a string of markets. Forty years later a British newspaper acknowledged his entrepreneurial skills by naming him Man of the Year. A journalist interviewed the country boy-turned-tycoon. "Well, sir, what did you think when you read the announcement that you were Man of the Year?"

"The truth is, I can't read. Or write."

The journalist was stunned. "And yet you've built a retail empire. Was that your goal from the beginning?"

"Actually no," said the tycoon. "What I really wanted was the bookkeeping job in a whorehouse."

Variations: European folklore is filled with stories of young men plucked from obscurity by chance. The most common story tells of military recruiting officers who see a muscular young man plowing a field—without a horse. They sign him up for the army of the king/emperor/tsar, and the boy becomes a military hero. In an American version, Minnesota football coach Don Spears saw Bronko Nagurski plowing a field and asked for directions. Nagurski picked up the plow with one hand and pointed the way. Spears, of course, immediately signed up Nagurski for his team.

The Standard Bedbug Letter

This story has been circulating in Canada and the United States since the 1880s.

An elderly woman traveling by train from Buffalo to Pittsburgh was horrified to discover a bedbug in her berth. When she arrived home, she wrote a strongly worded letter of complaint to the president of the railroad.

To her delight she received a reply, two pages long, just a few days later. On the first page, the president offered an abject apology and assured her that he would attend to this breach of sanitation personally.

The elderly woman was very pleased with the president's letter and turned to the second page. It was a handwritten note that read, "Send this cranky old bitch the standard bedbug letter."

Traveling Companions

The CEO of a Canadian airline that specialized in business travel was concerned that his company was not doing enough for its female travelers. To gauge how the airline served women business passengers, the CEO inaugurated a new company policy that encouraged employees to take their wives on all of their business trips. Furthermore, the human resources department kept a file of all employees who traveled with their wives.

Three months into the new program, the airline sent the wives a detailed questionnaire about their flight experiences. When the responses had been tabulated, it was found that 90 percent of the wives had answered something along the lines of, "What business trips? My husband never took me on any of his business trips."

Variations: In an alternate version of this story, American Airlines distributes 200 blank airline tickets to their employees so wives can accompany their husbands on business flights. A follow-up of the program finds that none of the women whose names appeared on the 200 tickets were wives of the business travelers.

The Unexpected Bequest

A botanist traveled to Honduras to study rare tropical plants. One day, while driving along a dusty road, he passed a cemetery where a very poorly attended funeral was in progress. Only a priest and another man in a black suit stood beside the grave. But atop the casket was a large arrangement of extremely rare orchids. The botanist pulled into the cemetery and joined the priest and the lone mourner.

When the prayers were concluded, the mourner took the botanist aside and asked him if he would join him in the cemetery's office for a moment.

Once they were inside, the man introduced himself. "I am the late Señor Ortiz's attorney. My client was very wealthy, but he was a difficult man to get along with. He made an stipulation in his will that if anyone other than the priest and myself attended his funeral, that person should receive a bequest of a $100,000 dollars."

The botanist was stunned. He didn't know what to say.

"If you come with me to my office in the city, I can write you a check. I know this must come as a shock. So is there anything I can get you now?" said the attorney.

"Yes," said the botanist. "Can I have that bouquet of orchids?"

Variations: In the most common alternate version of this legend, two men stop at an inn. Both make love to the hostess that night. One tells her that he was flattered that such a lovely woman took an interest in him, while the other proves to be a lout. A year later, a lawyer contacts the grateful lover to inform him that the innkeeper has died and left her considerable fortune to him.

The Leopard in the Luggage

A sheep farmer in the Transvaal of South Africa was having a terrible time. A leopard was killing his sheep. Every night the farmer set out new and ever more ingenious traps, but the leopard eluded them all. Finally, he called in a professional trapper. The trapper knew that the farmer was desperate and he charged an exorbitant sum. Still, the sheep farmer saw no alternative.

The next morning, the farmer went out to his pasture and there was the leopard, caught in the trap. He ran to the house for his tranquilizer gun, shot the leopard and then got out his knife to slit its throat.

But as he stood over the animal he thought about its rarity and beauty. He couldn't bring himself to kill it, so he resolved to take it to a wildlife preserve instead.

The only trouble with this noble thought was that the farmer had no cage to transport a wild leopard. In fact, the only container he had around his place that was big enough for the animal was a large steamer trunk. It would have to do.

He wrestled the unconscious beast into the trunk, punched some air holes in it, locked it and then tied it with heavy rope. Somehow, he managed to get the trunk into the back of his truck.

When the job was done, he rewarded himself with a pint of cold beer. Then he set off on the long drive to the wildlife preserve.

An hour later, the sheep farmer felt the call of nature and pulled over to the side of the road to relieve himself. As he stepped out of the truck, he heard the leopard yawn. It wouldn't be long before the animal was fully awake. The sheep farmer scurried into the bushes to complete his business. A few minutes later, he stepped out of the brush just in time to see another truck pulling away—with his trunk in the back.

The farmer was furious and was about to give chase when he recalled what was inside the trunk. He imagined what would happen to the thieves when they opened the trunk. So, with a contented smile on his face, the farmer turned his truck around and drove home.

The New Ambassador

The ambassador from a newly independent nation in Eastern Europe traveled to Paris for an international conference. It was the first time his country would be counted among the nations of Europe and the ambassador was intent upon making a good impression. Consequently, he arrived in Paris a few days early and purchased several beautifully tailored suits and a fine wool overcoat.

On the day of the conference, he entered the Palais de Luxembourg to find that he alone had come wearing an overcoat. Nervous and self-conscious, the ambassador looked around for a place where he could check his coat. Standing beside the door to the anteroom, he saw a distinguished-looking gentleman in a black suit.

The relieved ambassador walked over and handed the man his

coat, but the man would not take it.

"Why will you not take my coat?" the ambassador demanded.

"Because I am not a valet," the man replied indignantly. "I am the Prime Minister of France."

The Chatty Employee

The CEO of a large corporation in Kansas City was convinced that every time he walked along the corridors of his headquarters, more employees were chatting than working. He decided to take drastic measures to correct this failing.

The CEO called a company-wide meeting in the auditorium and announced that he would no longer tolerate idle chatter during work hours. Then he waved a stack of checks over his head and said, "I have checks here, all of them made out to *Cash* in the amount of two thousand dollars. That will be your severance pay if I find any of you talking when you should be working."

Then the CEO dismissed his employees. After lunch, he made a tour of his headquarters. Every office was silent and all of the employees were quietly doing their work. Except one. In the human resources department, he found a man chatting away to the vice president of personnel.

"Didn't I say I would get rid of anyone I found talking? Now take your two thousand dollars and get out of here!"

The man looked stunned at first, but he accepted the check and left the office without a word.

"Some fools don't know what's good for them," the CEO said. Then, turning to the vice president, he said, "By the way, who was that guy?"

"He was a job applicant," the vice president said quietly.

The Unexpected Escort

A newly divorced woman from a wealthy town in Connecticut was going to a posh charity ball. She wanted to make an impression on her friends, so she called an escort service and insisted upon speaking to the manager.

"This is an extremely important engagement for me and I want the best you have," she said. "He must be over six feet tall, very handsome and between thirty and thirty-five years old."

"We have several men who fit that description," the manager said.

"And there's one more thing," the woman said. "He mustn't be Jewish."

"I promise you," the manager said. "The escort I send you will not be Jewish."

A week later, on the evening of the charity ball, the woman opened her front door. There stood a tall, devastatingly handsome black man.

"Good evening," he said. "I'm from the escort service."

The woman stammered, "No. There must be some mistake."

"That's not possible, ma'am. Mr. Shapiro never makes a mistake."

Awake at His Own Wake

A funeral director in New Jersey received a call informing him that an elderly man had died quietly in his bed. The director sent his newest assistant out to collect the body. "And remember," the director said, "when you get back here, lean on the corpse's stomach to let all the air out."

Two days later, the family filed into the funeral home for the wake. The body was laid out in a handsome casket with banks of flowers all around. The funeral director was certain the family would be pleased. He himself escorted the widow forward so she could inspect her husband.

They had just arrived at the casket when the body began to tremble. Then it sat bolt upright in the casket. The family members screamed, while the widow shrieked and fell into a dead faint on the floor.

A few minutes later, the widow came to on the couch in the funeral director's private study. "He's alive!" she screamed. "Cosmo's alive!"

"No, no," the funeral director said. "You're husband's not alive. He was just suffering from a little gas."

Give the Guy a Hand

Whenever surgeons at a Long Island hospital had to perform an amputation, they always called upon two new interns to get rid of the severed limb. The interns were getting pretty tired of the job, so one day when they were assigned the disposal of a man's left arm, one of the interns had an idea.

He took a shirt from his locker, tore off its left sleeve and put it on the severed arm. Then he sutured a $20 bill to the hand.

"Let's go for a ride," he said to his friend.

They drove off toward New York City. When they got to the first tollbooth, the driver held out the severed arm with the $20 bill attached to it. As the tollbooth clerk held out his hand for the money, the intern let go of the arm and said, "Keep the whole thing. It's yours."

Then he hit the gas.

ELVIS'S MOTORCYCLE AND OTHER CELEBRITY RUMORS

ELVIS'S MOTORCYCLE AND OTHER CELEBRITY RUMORS

Elvis's Motorcycle

A man went to an outdoor flea market near his home in Indiana and found a beat-up vintage Harley-Davidson motorcycle. After some spirited negotiation with the seller, he got the price down to $600 and took the motorcycle home.

The next day, the new owner went to a Harley dealer and requested the parts he would need to restore the bike. He and the dealer started talking, and the dealer mentioned that he collected vintage Harleys.

"Do you collect?" the dealer asked.

"Nope. But when I saw this bike, I felt that I had to buy it."

"You don't say. What's so special about this Harley?"

"The color's strange. It's a funny shade of blue. In fact, the first time I saw it, the Elvis song, 'Blue Suede Shoes' popped into my head."

The dealer was silent for a moment. Then he said, "Blue is a pretty unusual color for a Harley. I'd like to see this bike."

"I could bring it by this afternoon."

"I'll be here."

After lunch, the man returned with his blue Harley. The dealer looked the bike over closely. His hand seemed to tremble a little when he placed it on the seat cushion.

"I've got to tell you. This is one rare Harley. I could offer you... oh, let's say ... $75,000."

The Harley's owner took a deep breath. "Well, I'm kinda attached to this bike. But since you're a collector, let's say $125,000."

"That would be fair if the bike were in mint condition. But it's a little beat up. The best I could do is $100,000."

For appearances' sake, the owner hesitated before he said, "You've got a deal."

That night, inside his locked garage, the dealer removed the bike's seat and held it up to a light. Engraved on the underside was the inscription he knew would be there: "To Elvis, from James Dean."

The dealer sold the Harley at an auction for $4 million.

Variations: A motorcycle enthusiast finds the beat-up bike in a barn at an estate sale. In an effort to track down parts for it, he calls the Harley-Davidson customer service number and gives them the bike's serial number. His call is transferred to a vice president of the corporation, who tells the collector that the company will give him a quarter of a million dollars for the bike. In another version, the bike was a gift to Elvis from his wife, Priscilla.

James Dean's Car

James Dean died on September 30, 1955, when his new Porsche Spyder crashed head-on into another car. After the accident, a secondhand car dealer purchased the wrecked Porsche. He planned to put it on display and charge admission. But when a flatbed truck delivered the car to the dealer's lot, it rolled off and broke a mechanic's legs. Spooked, the dealer decided to strip the Porsche and sell it for parts.

A Beverly Hills doctor bought the Dean engine and had it installed in his Porsche. The doctor was killed in a crash the first time he took his car out.

Another physician in southern California bought the Dean transmission. He was killed when the transmission locked in fifth gear and the Porsche hurled itself through a guardrail and into a ravine.

A New Yorker bought two of the Dean tires. The first time he took his Porsche out on the road, both of the tires blew out at the same time. The car flipped over, crushing the driver.

An auto museum in Salinas, California, purchased the body of the Dean car. But as it was being transported there, the driver of the truck lost control of his vehicle, skidded off the highway and was killed.

No one knows what became of all of these cursed auto parts. One story claims that they were collected again, crushed and buried in a landfill near the Mexican border.

Elvis Lives!

The Elvis faithful claim to have spotted their King everywhere from rooms that are off-limits to tourists at Graceland to the K-Mart in Kalamazoo, Michigan. And they've collected the data that proves Elvis is still alive.

• Two days before his alleged death, Elvis telephoned a friend named Foster to tell her he would cancel his upcoming tour. Miss Foster was surprised and asked if Elvis was ill. "I'm fine," he said. "In fact, I feel better now than I have in a long time. My troubles will soon be over. But remember this: Don't believe anything you read about me over the next few days." Then Elvis hung up.

• Two hours after Elvis's death was announced to the public, a man who bore a striking resemblance to the King showed up at the Memphis airport and purchased a plane ticket to Buenos Aires. The traveler paid cash and gave his name as "John Burrows," the alias Elvis always used when he was on tour.

• Elvis's full name is Elvis Aron Presley. He and his family were always sticklers for the unconventional spelling of his middle name. Yet his gravestone bears the incorrect spelling, "Aaron."

• Toward the end of his life, one of the King's favorite books was the spiritual autobiography of a Hindu yogi who urged his followers to relinquish wealth and fame and find peace in obscurity. Did Elvis abandon stardom to find spiritual serenity in the out-of-the-way town of Kalamazoo?

Paul Is Dead

One of the great legends of the late 1960s was the rumor that Paul McCartney was dead. Believers found clues in the Beatles's album covers and in the songs.

• The cover of *Abbey Road* was interpreted as a kind of funeral procession. John, dressed all in white, represents the minister; Ringo, in a dark suit, is the undertaker; George, in a denim work shirt, is the gravedigger; and Paul, in a suit but barefoot (because, supposedly, that is how they bury bodies in England) is the corpse.

• The *Abbey Road* album cover shot shows a car parked on the street. Its license plate reads "28 IF," meaning Paul would be 28 if he were still alive.

• If the *Sgt. Pepper's Lonely Hearts Club Band* album is held to a mirror, the characters on the drum in front of Paul read "HE DIE."

• On Paul's Sgt. Pepper uniform is an arm patch with the initials OPD, for "Officially Pronounced Dead."

• At the end of "Strawberry Fields Forever," John can be heard saying, "I buried Paul."

• Play "Revolution 9" backwards and the phrase "number nine, number nine" becomes "Turn me on, dead man."

Tupac Lives!

Fans of gangsta rapper Tupac Shakur have uncovered a host of clues and inconsistencies to prove that Tupac faked his death.

• Tupac always wore a bulletproof vest. It is inconceivable that he would have gone to so public an event as the Mike Tyson fight without protection.

• Not long before the shooting, Tupac told interviewers that he wanted to step out of the limelight. "But the only way I could pull it off," he said, "is if people think I'm dead."

• Tupac's funeral was canceled for unknown reasons.

• The cover of *The 7 Day Theory* album shows Tupac crucified and bleeding from five bullet wounds. Is this a clue that he is planning a resurrection?

• The only witness to the shooting, Yafeu Fula (Kadafi of the Outlawz), was gunned down in an apartment building hallway in East Orange, New Jersey, not long after Tupac was shot. Was he about to blow Tupac's cover?

• "R U Still Down" was released under the name "2Pac." Does this mean Tupac is back?

Saving Richard Nixon

In the late 1970s, after his resignation from the presidency, Richard Nixon retired to his beachfront home in San Clemente, California. The house was on one of the hottest surfing spots in southern California. But the land was private property, and the former president would not give the public access to it.

One day Nixon went swimming alone. The riptide caught him, and he began to call frantically for help. Two surfers who were illegally on the beach heard his cries. They swam out on their boards and rescued the former president.

Once he was safely on the beach, Nixon said, "Boys, you've saved my life. Whatever you want, if it's in my power to give, you can have it."

One of the surfers said, "Open the beach to the public."

"Done," said Nixon. Then turning to the other surfer he asked, "Now what would you like?"

The other surfer said, "Can I have a burial plot in Arlington National Cemetery?"

"Yes, I could arrange that," said the former president. "But why do you want such a thing?"

"Because," the surfer said, "when my dad finds out I saved the life of Richard Nixon, he's going to kill me."

Two Legends from Johnny Carson's *Tonight Show*

One of the most famous legends from the 1960s involves an appearance by golfer Arnold Palmer on Johnny Carson's *Tonight Show*.

During the interview, Carson asked Palmer if he had any superstitions or rituals he performed before a tournament.

"Yes," said Palmer. "The night before a tournament, my wife kisses each of my balls."

Carson said, "That will make your putter stutter."

In another *Tonight Show* legend, Burt Reynolds mentions that he has just won a massive judgment against AT&T. Part of the settlement is unlimited free phonecalls. So the generous star reads off his calling card number and invites all of his fans to reach out and touch someone at AT&T's expense.

Variations: The most common variation on the putter legend is that it was Mrs. Palmer who was being interviewed by Carson. Lately, the legend has been updated so that Palmer is being interviewed by Jay Leno. The details of the calling card legend are remarkably consistent, only the name of the celebrity changes—to Steve McQueen, Paul Newman or Sammy Davis, Jr.

Michael Jackson's Telephone Number

When Michael Jackson's megahit album *Thriller* premiered in

December 1984, the first seven digits of the product number in the bar code were rumored to be the Gloved One's phone number.

A spokesman for Epic Records in Los Angeles denied the rumor that one could reach Jackson by dialing the code numbers. But people tried anyway—as the stylists at a hair salon in Bellevue, Washington, know. They were getting an average of 50 calls a day for Jackson.

The Bozo No-No

Bozo the Clown was a popular kids' TV show in the late 1950s and early 1960s. The program was filmed live, with children who had written in for tickets joining Bozo on stage and playing a variety of games.

One day, the contest was a race carrying an egg in a spoon. When one little boy dropped his egg halfway across the stage, he said, "Shit!"

Bozo hurried over, put his hand on the little guy's shoulder, and said in his most cheerful voice, "That's a Bozo no-no!"

To which the kid replied, "Ram it, clownie!"

The Anxious Tourists

Two elderly ladies who had never traveled out of their home state, Iowa, decided they needed a little excitement in their lives. So they asked a travel agent to arrange a week in New York City.

When they landed at La Guardia Airport, two flight attendants walked them to the baggage claim area. "Now be careful in the city," one of the attendants said. "Always hold on tightly to your handbag."

"And avoid the subway," said the other attendant. "Cabs are more expensive, but they are the safest way to get around town."

The limo driver who took the ladies to their hotel in Midtown had some advice, too. "If you do run into trouble, just do what the man says and you won't get hurt."

Naturally, all of this advice made the two out-of-towners a little apprehensive. But after a day or two of sightseeing without any unpleasant incidents, the ladies decided that New York City was not such a frightening place after all.

Their travel agent had made dinner reservations for them at the Rainbow Room in Rockefeller Center. Feeling bolder, the ladies decided to walk the four blocks from their hotel to the restaurant. But after a block or two, they became uneasy. A very tall, broad-shouldered black man with a rottweiler was following them. "Let's walk a little faster," said one of the ladies. "Once we're on the elevator, he can't follow us."

So the two friends picked up their pace, hurried through the revolving doors and scurried across the lobby to the bank of elevators that would take them up to the Rainbow Room. As the elevator doors opened, they could hear the man and the dog entering the lobby.

"Hurry! Push the close button!" one of the women said to the other.

But as the doors began to shut, two strong hands reached in and pried them apart. The man and the dog got on the elevator. He hit the button for the penthouse.

There was no place for the ladies to go. They backed into a corner of the elevator car, clutching their handbags and looking nervously at the rottweiler that sniffed at their feet.

Suddenly the man said, "Sit, Lady!"

Both women plopped down on the floor.

At that moment, the elevator came to a stop and the doors opened onto the lobby of the Rainbow Room. The man with the dog called to the hostess, "Could you help these ladies to their feet and escort them to their table."

"We were so frightened," one of the ladies confided to the hostess. "He shouted, 'Sit lady!' and we did just what he said."

"Oh, ma'am. The gentleman wasn't talking to you," the hostess replied. "He was just giving a command to his dog. His dog's name is Lady."

"But how do you know all this?" the other lady asked.

"The gentleman lives in the penthouse. We see him and his dog all the time. Didn't you recognize him? That was Michael Jordan."

Variations: Over the years, the black celebrity the ladies fail to recognize has changed, depending on who is most prominent at the moment. Earlier versions of this legend feature Reggie Jackson, Eddie Murphy and Mike Tyson.

A Good Samaritan Gets His Reward

Late on a cold, rainy night in November, a factory worker was driving home along I-95 in Connecticut when he saw a well-dressed man standing beside a limo on the shoulder of the road. The man was trying to flag down passing traffic, but no one stopped. So the factory worker pulled over.

"What's the problem?" he asked as the driver of the limo ran up to his car.

"The ignition's dead," the limo driver said. "And so is our cell phone. Could you give me a lift to a service station so I can get a tow?"

"Sure. Hop in. There's a station about five minutes from here."

The factory worker took the driver to the station, waited while he arranged for roadside service, drove him back to the limo and waited again until the guys from service station arrived.

"You've been great," the driver said. "My boss would like to thank you."

The limo door opened and a tall man in a cashmere coat stepped out onto the rainy highway. "I'm Donald Trump. My wife and I want to express our appreciation. You've gone to a lot of trouble on our behalf. Is there something I can do for you?"

For a moment, the factory worker was stunned to meet one of the wealthiest men in America, but he recovered quickly. "Sure," he said. "There's one thing. Send my wife flowers. My wife would love to get flowers from Donald Trump."

"My pleasure," said the Donald. "Just write your wife's name and address here." He handed the man a leatherbound notepad and a gold pen.

Then they shook hands, and everyone continued on their way.

The next morning, while the factory worker and his wife were having coffee, the doorbell rang. It was a florist delivering a massive flower arrangement. The note attached to the flowers read, "With best wishes and profound appreciation from Donald and Ivana Trump. P.S.: We've paid off your mortgage."

Variations: In earlier versions of this legend, the good Samaritan stops to help the wife of a celebrity—Mrs. Nat King Cole, Mrs. Perry Como or Mrs. Leon Spinks. The reward is a pair of free tickets for a sold-out concert or prizefight.

The Unrecognized Celebrity

The vicar of a village church in England made a habit of visiting newcomers to the parish. He heard that a man had moved into the neighborhood, so he dropped by.

"Good morning. My name is Edmund Barset. I am the vicar here, and I wanted to welcome you to the village."

The man at the door smiled. "Call me Eric. Please come in, Vicar."

In the parlor, the vicar saw several guitars.

"Do you play?"

"A little," said Eric.

"I say, we're having an entertainment to benefit the building restoration fund. I don't suppose you'd consider playing for us?"

"Well…." the man said slowly.

Thinking that he needed a little reassurance, the vicar said, "Oh, you mustn't be nervous. I'm sure you're a fine musician. Maybe just a little more practice. The entertainment is not for two months. That should give you plenty of time to prepare, don't you think?"

"Yes it would," Eric said. "I'd be happy to play."

"Right. Very good. Well, I'll drop by with the details another time."

"That will be fine," Eric said, as he saw the vicar to the door.

Two months later, the villagers gathered for the benefit. They heard Eric Clapton, unplugged, in their parish hall.

Variations: Other versions of this legend feature a woman at an airport who mistakes a star from the NFL or the NBA for a porter, or American tourists at a historic villa in Europe who mistake a casually dressed film star for the gardener. The names of the athletes and the film stars change depending on who is popular at the time.

The Nervous Stargazer

A woman visiting Los Angeles walked into an ice cream store one afternoon. As she browsed along the case filled with different flavors, she noticed a man at the counter. Once she made her selection and walked over to the counter to order, she realized that the man was Jack Nicholson.

"Be cool," she told herself. "This is L.A. The town is full of celebrities."

A clerk asked if he could take her order.

"Uh . . . Ice cream. I want ice cream. In a cone? Do you have ice cream cones here? Of course you do. What am I saying? This is an ice cream store. Every ice cream store has ice cream cones. Which is good. Because that's what I want.

"I'm babbling. But I'm going to stop now. There. See? Now I've stopped babbling. Now I can order. I'll have chocolate chip. Two scoops. I mean a double. On an ice cream cone. Or do you say in an ice cream cone? Whatever. I want a cone with two scoops of chocolate chip. Ice cream. Please. Thank you so very much."

The clerk went to make the woman's cone while another clerk filled pints of various kinds of ice cream for Jack Nicholson.

The poor woman wanted to remain calm, but it was hopeless. The proximity of Jack Nicholson was making her jumpy. She knew she had made a fool of herself. All she wanted was her cone so she could get out of the store.

After what seemed like an eternity, the clerk returned with her cone. She paid and walked out. But on the street, she realized that she did not have her ice cream cone. As she stared at her empty hands, Jack Nicholson came out of the store with two large bags. He leaned over the woman's shoulder and whispered in her ear, "The cone's in your purse."

John Carradine's Screen Test

This legend has been making the rounds in Hollywood for nearly 70 years.

John Barrymore was a Hollywood star in the 1930s. When he learned that his friend John Carradine wanted to move from the stage to the screen, Barrymore offered to help.

"This will be very simple," he told Carradine. "I've reserved a studio for your screen test. It will be me and the crew. No directors, no producers. No one who might make you nervous."

"This is more than decent of you," Carradine said.

"Not at all. Now here's what you have to do. I want you to step through that door there and pantomime a man who has just had a tremendously satisfying meal. No words, just gestures."

"I love it," said Carradine, as he vanished behind the door.

"Ready, John?"

"Ready!"

"Then . . . action!"

Carradine stepped out in front of the camera, a smile of perfect contentment on his face. He ran his tongue over his lips. He wiped his mouth with his handkerchief. He stroked his belly. He even gave a modest burp.

"Cut!" said Barrymore. "Print! Superb, John. Exactly what I was hoping for."

Carradine beamed.

"Tomorrow we'll show it to the studio heads together."

The next morning, Carradine, Barrymore and the studio's top executives assembled in a private screening room.

Carradine's performance was perfect. Every gesture and facial expression confirmed that here was a man who had just eaten something delectable.

Carradine thought the clip was over, but then the camera cut back to the door. Now John Barrymore stepped in front of the camera—zipping up his fly.

Bill Gates is the Antichrist

Many people in the computer industry believe that Bill Gates of Microsoft is evil incarnate. But one hardworking hacker has proven that Bill Gates is the devil himself—or least one of his really close subordinates.

Gates's full name is William Henry Gates III. If you convert the letters of Bill Gates (the name he goes by these days) to their ASCII numerical values and add the III, you get the following:

B	66	G	71	I	1
I	73	A	65	I	1
L	76	T	84	I	1
L	76	E	69		
		S	83		

The total is 666, the number of the Beast in the book of Revelation.

Short Takes

• Charlie Chaplin once anonymously entered a Charlie Chaplin look-alike contest. He lost.

• At the end of his career George Reeves, who played Superman in the television series, believed he could fly. He died when he leapt from a tall building in a single bound.

• The Gerber Baby is a portrait of the infant Humphrey Bogart, drawn by his mother.

• Marilyn Monroe was the model for Tinker Bell in the Disney animated cartoon version of *Peter Pan*.

• When he died, Walt Disney was frozen in liquid nitrogen in the hope that at some future date, medical technology would be able to bring him back to life.

• Barbra Streisand made her film debut in a porn flick.

• "Mama" Cass Elliot of the Mamas and the Papas choked to death on a ham sandwich. At the time of her death, she was pregnant with John Lennon's child.

• Fred Rogers of *Mister Rogers' Neighborhood* was a sniper in Vietnam.

• Jerry "the Beaver" Mathers of *Leave It to Beaver* was killed in Vietnam.

• Pia Zadora once appeared in the title role of *The Diary of Anne Frank*. Her performance was so terrible that when the Nazis arrived, someone in the audience cried out, "She's in the attic!"

• James Dean did not die in a car crash, but was horribly disfigured. He has lived as a recluse ever since.

• John F. Kennedy did not die of his bullet wounds, but survives in a coma in a secret room of a Dallas nursing home.

• Bruce Lee was killed by Chinese martial arts masters who were angry with him for teaching their ancient secrets to Westerners.

• Bruce Lee was killed by Hong Kong crime lords who were angry with him for refusing to work in their films.

• Brandon Lee, Bruce Lee's son, was murdered by Chinese martial arts masters or Hong Kong crime lords who were pursuing their vendetta into the next generation.

• The actual footage of the fatal shooting of Brandon Lee was left in the final cut of *The Crow*.

• After the show's final episode, the cast of *Green Acres* threw a farewell dinner in which the pig, Arnold Ziffel, was the main course.

• John Wayne turned down the role of Matt Dillon on *Gunsmoke*.

• Albert Einstein guest-starred on *Gunsmoke*.

• Charles Manson auditioned for the Monkees.

• Offended by the portrayal of Buckwheat, Bill Cosby bought the rights to *The Little Rascals* so the series would never appear on television again.

• At the 1992 Academy Awards, the Best Actress award was

supposed to go to Vanessa Redgrave for her performance in *Howard's End*. But presenter Jack Palance was too confused or drunk (depending on which version you hear) to read the card. He could make out nominee Marisa Tomei's name on the teleprompter, however, so he announced that she had won the Oscar.

• Burt Reynolds is Tom Selleck's father.

• Clark Gable is Tom Selleck's father.

• During one of his concerts Ozzy Osborne, the *really* bad boy of rock 'n' roll, bit off the head of a live bat.

• Andrew Cunanan, who murdered fashion designer Gianni Versace and several other men, faked his own death and is now at large masquerading as a woman.

ALLIGATORS IN THE SEWERS AND OTHER CLASSIC URBAN LEGENDS

ALLIGATORS IN THE SEWERS AND OTHER CLASSIC URBAN LEGENDS

Alligators in the Sewers

The New York Times *first reported alligators in the city's sewer system in the 1920s.*

At one time, the hottest item in Florida's souvenir shops were baby alligators. But the trouble with baby alligators is that they grow up to be adult alligators—an inevitability which generally occurred to the tourists within a week or so of their arrival back home. Some owners gave their alligators to the zoo. But in New York City the preferred method of getting rid of an unwanted baby alligator was simply to flush it down the toilet.

The alligators thrived in the sewers of New York. There were plenty of rats and raw garbage to feed on. And for variety, an alligator would sometimes catch an unwary sanitation worker.

Over several generations, the New York alligators have evolved into a distinct species. Because they never see the sun, the alligators are all albinos.

Spanish Fly and the Stick Shift

Two high school sophomores in Tennessee had been going steady for three months. While the boy wanted to have sex, his girlfriend absolutely refused to go to bed with him.

"If I don't get something soon," he complained to his friends, "I'm going to explode."

Then one morning, a senior came up to the boy in the hallway outside the chemistry lab. "Hey kid! The story is your girlfriend won't play nice."

"What business is that of yours?"

"Calm down, buddy," the senior said. "I've got a solution. It so happens that I have a little something that will get your girlfriend in the mood. Ever hear of Spanish fly?"

"You've got Spanish fly? That would solve my problem!"

"Easy does it, Romeo. For fifty bucks, I can give you enough so you can keep your girlfriend in the mood from now until you kids graduate. Bring me the money tomorrow and your troubles are over."

The next day, the boy met the senior under the bleachers on the football field. "Just remember, kid. A little of this stuff goes a long way. Put a tiny pinch in her soda and she'll be all over you."

"I'll remember," the boy said. "And thanks!"

On Friday night the boy took his girlfriend to a drive-in movie. When he went to the refreshment stand, he poured a tiny bit of the aphrodisiac in his girlfriend's soda. But when he considered how horny he felt and how determined his girlfriend was, he decided that more was better. He dumped a handful of the powder in her drink, stirred it with a straw and walked as casually as he could back to the car.

He handed his girlfriend her drink. "I'm so thirsty," she said. She took a long drink. Then she said, "You forgot the french fries!"

"I'll go back," the boy said. "It will only take a minute."

But there was a long line at the refreshment stand now, and 20 minutes passed before he returned with the french fries. As he approached the car, he saw that a crowd had gathered. And his car was rocking violently. He pushed his way through the spectators and opened the door. There was his girlfriend on her knees, crying out in ecstasy as she made passionate love to the car's gearshift.

The Psycho Upstairs

A high school girl was babysitting two little kids for a neighbor when the phone rang. When she answered, a man's voice said, "You better get out of the house before I come down there and kill you."

The girl hung up without saying a word. "It's just some psycho," she told herself, and went back to watching television.

Fifteen minutes later, the phone rang again.

"Hello?"

"You better get out of the house now. I'm going to come down there and kill you."

"Stop calling me, you sick freak!" the babysitter shouted into the phone, and slammed it down.

But before she could get back to the couch, the phone rang a third time. It was the same voice on the other end.

"I warned you. I've killed the kids. And I'm gonna kill you."

Now the babysitter was frightened. She hung up, called the police and told them the story.

"We're sending a squad car over now, miss," said the officer. "But please hold so we can trace where the last three calls to your number came from."

A moment later the officer came back on the line, "Get out of the house now! Those calls came from the upstairs phone!"

Variations: In another version of this popular urban legend, two high school girls are babysitting together. Frightened by the phone calls, one goes upstairs to check on the kids and is stabbed by a killer lurking in the children's room. Before she dies, she manages to scream out to her friend, "The children are dead! The killer is coming for you! Get out of the house!"

The Poodle in the Microwave

A woman in Arkansas adored her miniature poodle. She took the poodle with her everywhere. She cooked all its meals herself and knitted it little outfits to wear in cold weather. She even bought it a pink leather collar studded with rhinestones.

So it broke her heart every week when she had to wash the poodle. No matter how thoroughly the woman dried the dog, it trembled violently for hours afterward until the last little bit of moisture had evaporated from its coat.

The woman had tried hairdryers, but the noise terrified the poodle and the hot air dried out its skin. It seemed hopeless.

Then one day the woman bought a microwave oven. And that's when she had an idea. If the microwave could heat up food in minutes, it could certainly dry Fluffy in the same amount of time.

On bath day she shampooed the dog and carried the trembling little creature into the kitchen. She popped open the door of the microwave and placed the dog inside. She shut the door securely and programmed the oven to eight minutes on high. Then she went back to the bathroom to clean out the tub.

Before she had finished, she heard an explosion. As she rushed downstairs, she recognized the aroma of cooked meat. To her horror, she found the microwave door blown off its hinges and bits of cooked poodle strewn all over her kitchen.

Curses! Broiled Again!

Over the Christmas and New Year's holiday, a South Dakota woman took a vacation in Miami. She returned home to the frozen north with a magnificent tan. But within a few days, the tan began to fade.

"I'm not going to be pale all winter long," she vowed, so she scheduled an appointment at the local tanning salon. But one 15-minute session on the tanning bed seemed to make no difference. She returned again the next day. And the next. And the day after that. It was no good. Daily 15-minute sessions were not restoring the deep golden tan she had acquired in Florida.

"I'd like to schedule a two-hour session for tomorrow," she told the young woman at the counter.

"But ma'am, we're not allowed to do that. Fifteen minutes is the limit. It's the law. The health department would shut us down."

"That's absurd. If I can lie out for two hours in the sun, I should be able to use your tanning beds just as long."

But arguing got her nowhere. The tanning salon would not let her tan for longer than 15 minutes.

The next morning, the woman had an idea. She got out the phone book and tore out the page that listed all the tanning salons in a 100-mile radius. She visited ten tanning salons that day and twelve more the next day. She was very pleased with the results. Thanks to her tanning marathon, she was darker than she had ever been in her life.

On the third day, however, when she woke up, the woman felt

very strange. She made an appointment with her doctor. He was surprised by the darkness of her tan. "Where have you been?" he asked.

She told him of her little scheme to sidestep the 15-minute limit. "So I expect I'm just a little dehydrated. That used to happen when I was in Miami," she said.

"We'll just run some tests to find out."

An hour or so later, the doctor called the woman into his office. "I really wish you had not gone to all those tanning salons," the doctor said.

"Why? Have I damaged my skin?"

"I wish that was all you'd done. I'm afraid you have about 24 hours to live. By spending all that time on the tanning beds, you cooked your internal organs."

Variations: Two common alternate versions of this story are slightly less grisly. In one version, only one arm was fried by prolonged tanning, but the arm had to be amputated. In the second version the young woman goes blind from her marathon tanning sessions.

The Vanishing Hitchhiker

Late one night in the early summer of 1980 a man was driving along a rural road in Missouri. Up ahead he could see a young man dressed in a tuxedo, hitchhiking.

The man pulled over and rolled down the window on the passenger side of his car. "Son, you always get this dressed up when you want a ride?"

"I was at my high school prom tonight, sir. But my car broke down after I dropped my girlfriend off. Yours is the first car I've seen all evening. Would you mind giving me a ride home?"

"It's no trouble," the driver said. "Hop in."

As they pulled back onto the road, the man asked, "So where do you live?"

"My folks have a farm about ten miles from here."

The boy gave the driver detailed directions on how to find his house. "There's a picket fence with an arched gate covered with yellow roses," the kid said. "They're in full bloom now."

The two travelers chatted pleasantly for the next couple of miles, but the closer they got to their destination, the more quiet the kid became. At last, he was not responding to conversation at all. The driver gave up and watched for the arched gateway covered with yellow roses.

Finally, he saw the fence and the rose-covered arch, just as the boy had described them. He parked in front of the gate, turned and said, "Well, you're home now. I hope your folks haven't been too worried."

But there was no one in the passenger seat. The boy in the tuxedo had disappeared. "That boy couldn't have fallen out of the car," the man said to himself. "I would have heard the car door." But just in case, he retraced his route back to the place where he'd picked up the boy. He saw no one. So he went back to the farm house.

The front porch light was on, so he knocked at the door. An elderly woman answered. "Yes?"

"Ma'am, about half an hour ago I picked up a high school boy in a tuxedo. He said his car had broken down after his prom and he asked me to take him to this house. But—and I know this sounds crazy—when I pulled up to your gate, the boy was gone. Is he inside? Did he slip out of the car when I wasn't looking?"

"I've been expecting you," the woman said. "That was my Harold you gave a ride to. He was killed in a car crash as he was driving home after his high school prom. That was 25years ago tonight. Every year he appears at the scene of the accident and asks a stranger to take him home. But he always vanishes before he gets here."

Variations: There are many variations on the Vanishing Hitchhiker urban legend. In some versions the hitchhiker is a young woman who asks to be dropped off at the gates of a cemetery, as in the case of "Resurrection Mary," a favorite urban legend in the Chicago area.

In a European legend, the driver picks up two women who have a flat tire. When he gets to their apartment building, the women have vanished and the doorman explains that they were tenants in the building, but were killed just three weeks earlier. Sometimes the hitchhiker delivers prophetic warnings, such as "Jesus is coming back to earth soon," or "Mount St. Helens is about to erupt again." There is even a reverse legend in which the hitchhiker is a living person who is picked up by a phantom truck driver named Big Joe. At the end of the ride, Big Joe drops the hitchhiker off at a truck stop with some change for coffee. Then Joe and his rig disappear. Inside the truck stop, the hitchhiker learns that Big Joe died when he swerved into a ditch rather than hit a stalled schoolbus filled with children.

The Runaway Grandmother

This story dates back at least to the 1970s and may have been the inspiration for a scene in the movie National Lampoon's Vacation.

A family from Fort Worth, Texas, decided to take a vacation in Mexico. Mom and dad, the kids and grandma all piled into the station wagon for a trip south of the border. Then one morning, the family awoke to find that Grandma had died in her sleep.

"We should call the authorities," the mother said.

"No way," said the father. "It will be weeks of red tape and filling out forms before the Mexican government releases my mother's body. And when they finally do let her go, it will cost me a fortune to ship her back to Fort Worth."

"So what's your solution?"

"I say we wrap her up in the picnic blanket, tie the body to the roof of the car and drive like hell for the border."

"I think you're nuts," the mother said. "But let's give it a try."

It was almost noon by the time the station wagon was packed and grandma had been secured to the roof. The family had missed breakfast, and as they didn't want to delay any longer they also skipped lunch. "We'll eat when we're back in Texas," the father promised.

After six hours of nonstop driving, however, they were still about 100 miles from the border. Now everyone needed a break, so the father pulled over to a roadside restaurant.

"What about Grandma?" the wife asked.

"She'll be fine where she is," the father answered.

An hour or so later, the family emerged from the restaurant. The station wagon was gone, and Grandma was gone with it.

The family notified the police in Mexico and Texas, but the car— and the body—were never recovered.

The Suspicious Birthday Boy

The owner of a construction firm suspected that his wife was cheating on him. On the morning of his birthday, as he was driving a truck full of fresh cement to a new construction site, he decided to take a detour. He turned down his street, and sure enough, the drapes in his bedroom were drawn, and parked in front of his house was a shiny new BMW convertible.

The humiliated husband was enraged. "The cheap little tramp has the nerve to cheat on me on my own birthday!"

He backed up the truck and when he was perfectly positioned, he began to pour cement into the BMW. As the car filled up, he leaned on the truck horn and shouted, "Come out and fight, you little weasel!"

The front door of his house swung open and his wife stepped outside. She stood on the front lawn watching. When the car was filled with wet cement, the husband climbed out of the truck and walked over to his wife.

"Where's your rich boyfriend?"

"I don't have a boyfriend."

"You don't have a boyfriend?"

"That's right. I don't have a boyfriend. And now you don't have the BMW convertible I bought you for your birthday."

"Beam Me Up, Scotty!"

A patient at a Des Moines hospital for the mentally disturbed was convinced that he was Captain James T. Kirk of the starship *Enterprise*. One night, he managed to slip past security and escape. When he was picked up the next day by the local police, he insisted that he was perfectly sane and was being held against his will in the hospital.

The officer who found the man said, "The hospital folks tell us you think you're Captain Kirk."

"That's a lie! I demand a hearing to prove that I'm sane."

A few days later, the patient, several doctors from the hospital and the police officer who picked the man up appeared before a judge. The judge asked the escaped patient his name, his address and his birth date. To all of these questions, the man gave the proper response.

Then the judge asked, "Sir, who is president of the United States?"

The escaped patient smiled and said, "Grover Cleveland."

The judge shuffled some papers on his desk, cleared his throat, and said, "For your own safety, I am sending you back to the hospital for a period of observation—"

But before the judge could finish, the man pulled his wallet out of his back pocket, flipped it open, and cried, "I'm in trouble down here! Beam me up, Scotty!"

Variation: In another version of this legend, the defendant is a young man convicted of drunk driving who shows his contempt for the court by pulling out his wallet and saying, "Beam me up, Scotty. There's no intelligent life here."

Unusual Vacation Photos

Four college guys from Michigan State pooled their money and rented a condo on the beach in Jamaica for spring b reak. The condo was luxurious. Booze was cheap. The beaches were packed with beautiful women. The guys were living the good life in paradise. And they got just a little too obnoxious about it—especially with the two stewards assigned to their condo, whom they kept calling "Boy."

On the third day of their vacation, the guys returned to their condo to find it ransacked. Everything was gone—except their tooth-brushes and a Leica camera.

American Express refunded their travelers' checks. The resort bought them new clothes and comped them on their meals and their bar tab. The boys were just grateful that at least they still had their camera.

Exhausted after their long day of running from office to office and filling out one form after another, the guys decided to crash early. They went back to their condo, brushed their teeth and went to bed.

When they returned to East Lansing, they sent the film out to be developed. A few hours later, they met in a bar off-campus to look at the photos. The first few pictures were shots of them on the beach and goofing around in Kingston.

But the next few pictures were different. They showed the two stewards from the condo, naked, with the guys' toothbrushes stuck up their butts.

Variations: In the most common alternate version of this legend, the vacationers are newlyweds. The element of the story that varies most often is the setting—Florida, the Caribbean, even Europe—depending upon the preference of whoever is telling the legend.

The Mexican Pet

A woman from Colorado was on vacation in San Diego when she decided to take a day trip to Tijuana, Mexico. She didn't enjoy herself much. The town was noisy, the traffic was terrible, and the shops were filled with cheap trinkets. She was about to get in her car to go back to San Diego when she saw a tiny gray creature hiding behind a dumpster.

"What a darling little Chihuahua puppy," she said to herself. "The poor thing looks lost and hungry."

She dug around in her purse for a mint and offered it to the animal. It crept out from behind the dumpster and took the mint from the woman's hand. It was dirty and had no collar, so the woman assumed that no one owned it.

"I think I'll have to take you home with me," she said. "I'll call you Poncho." She picked him up, put him in the back seat of her car, and drove back to San Diego.

In the hotel, she gave Poncho a bath, and ordered him a hamburger from room service. Then she went to a pet store and bought a cardboard carry-on box so she could take Poncho with her on the plane.

Back home in Fort Collins, the woman took Poncho to a veterinarian for his shots and a checkup.

"So what have we here?" the vet asked, pointing to the cardboard box.

As she opened the box, the woman said, "Doctor, I rescued the sweetest little Mexican Chihuahua when I was in Tijuana."

The vet glanced in the box and stepped back. "Lady, I'm afraid what you rescued is a little Mexican rat."

Short Takes

• The secret ingredient in the original formula of Coca-Cola was cocaine.

• If you drink Coke after you've eaten Pop Rocks candy, your stomach will explode. That's how little Mikey, the kid who would eat anything in the Life cereal commercial, died.

• Green M&Ms are an aphrodisiac.

• For recreational sex, you can't beat a swimming pool. The chlorine is a foolproof contraceptive.

• Nine months after its 1965 blackout, New York City had the biggest baby boom in its history.

• Poinsettias are poisonous. Every Christmas, several small children die from eating the plants.

• At Halloween, sadists slip razor blades into apples and give them to trick-or-treaters.

• Blue Star lick-and-stick tattoos are laced with LSD.

• The Beatles song "Lucy in the Sky with Diamonds" was really a secret code for the band's drug of choice at the time, LSD.

• The fastest way to sell your house is to bury a small statue of St. Joseph in the front lawn. Make sure the head is pointing toward the house.

• A dying boy in England is trying to break the Guinness record for getting the most get-well cards.

• A dying boy in England is trying to break the Guinness record for collecting the most business cards.A dying boy in England is trying to break the Guinness record for receiving the most e-mails.

• An aluminum manufacturer will donate an hour of dialysis to a sick child for every 1,000 aluminum can flip tops it receives.

ADD YOUR OWN URBAN LEGND. . .

ADD YOUR OWN URBAN LEGEND. . .

ADD YOUR OWN URBAN LEGEND. . .

ADD YOUR OWN URBAN LEGEND. . .

ADD YOUR OWN URBAN LEGEND. . .

ADD YOUR OWN URBAN LEGEND. . .

ADD YOUR OWN URBAN LEGEND. . .

ADD YOUR OWN URBAN LEGEND. . .